# BRAVE NEW WORDS

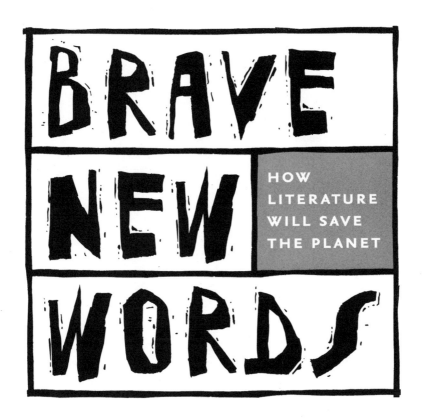

BRAVE NEW WORDS

HOW LITERATURE WILL SAVE THE PLANET

Elizabeth Ammons

UNIVERSITY OF IOWA PRESS

IOWA CITY

University of Iowa Press, Iowa City 52242

Copyright © 2010 by the University of Iowa Press

www.uiowapress.org

Printed in the United States of America

Design by April Leidig-Higgins

The University of Iowa Press is a member of Green Press Initiative and is committed to preserving natural resources.

Printed on acid-free paper

Library of Congress Cataloging-in-Publication Data
Ammons, Elizabeth.
Brave new words: how literature will save the planet / by Elizabeth Ammons.
      p.      cm.
ISBN-13: 978-1-58729-861-5 (pbk.)
ISBN-10: 1-58729-861-9 (pbk.)
      1. American literature — History and criticism — Theory, etc.    2. Social change — Philosophy.
3. Humanism — Social aspects.    4. Social problems in literature.    5. Social justice in literature.
6. Humanism in literature.    7. Literature and morals.    8. Literature and society.    I. Title.
PS169.S57A66    2010
810.9'35 — dc22                                   2009041320

Disconnection of body/mind/spirit is death-dealing. . . .
This disdain concept, this insidious and deadly virus,
still runs in the bloodstream of Western thought.
— Marilou Awiakta, *Selu*

# CONTENTS

# PREFACE

Unless I bury it in my backyard, the desktop computer on which I am writing will almost certainly end up in a mountain of toxic trash in Ghana. There, desperately poor children will strip it of tiny amounts of marketable metals and in the process destroy their health and drench the earth in poisons. I can pretend this reality does not exist. I can consider any response of mine futile. Or I can believe that human beings are capable of changing the world.

The activist tradition in American literature chooses the last of these three, as do the thinkers on whom I rely in the following pages. Although it is out of fashion in the academy to say so, words do have the power to transform people. That belief has motivated the progressive activist tradition in U.S. literature even when the situation has seemed most hopeless, and it continues to provide vision and strength in our own time of potentially disabling despair about global poverty and planetary devastation. Because this question of the future and of human beings' ability to remake the world matters for all life on the planet, I also emphasize that it is important to think about what young people are taught and how they are taught it.

This book is intended for general readers as well as my fellow teachers and scholars. As will become obvious, I believe an unnatural gap has opened between humanists in general — all people who turn to art, literature, history, philosophy, film, and comparative religions as important reservoirs of wisdom and inspiration — and professional humanists who work as literary scholars, people like myself who get paid to teach and write about literature. The gap is illustrated by a question I put to progressive people I know outside the academic world. What books of literary criticism do you especially like — not what literature do you like, but what books *about* literature and contemporary literary study? The answer, almost always, is a vacant stare. People read books by historians, philosophers, popular culture thinkers, art historians, religion scholars, political analysts, and biographers. But books about literature and contemporary thinking in the field? None — or none for the last twenty years, except perhaps a literary biography or two.

I think the failure of professional humanists to reach such an important audience suggests how irrelevant most literary inquiry has become. Too often the field consists of an insider's conversation that says little if anything at all to most people. It has in many instances lost sight of the real-world activist mission of much literature and of critics' responsibility to reach beyond narrow boundaries to speak to a general public. This book is addressed to present and future literature scholars and teachers who share my interest in breaking out of in-house performances for each other and wish to link their work directly to progressive activism.

This book also addresses readers outside academic settings. In my experience many people care intensely about altering the world in positive ways and are drawn to literature because, in addition to pleasure, they seek inspiration. Indeed, that is the message of this book. Progressive change begins in the human soul, not just the mind. Liberal activist writers in the United States have always known that. They have written in the past and they write today to insist on that truth and to inspire and fortify people in the collective struggle to achieve social justice and restore the earth. I am writing for general readers to encourage further awareness of this tradition and the vital issues and ideas that it contributes to the ongoing work of activist change.

For different readers, one chapter or another may be of more use or interest. The first, "Postmodern Fundamentalism," takes up the issue of belief in the postmodern world. While many progressive activists have not followed suit, as I point out, this chapter challenges much contemporary humanist thinking. Particularly in elite academic circles, it often (and ironically) joins forces with right-wing fundamentalism in labeling human agency impotent, earthly disaster unstoppable, and the future beyond our control. Against this nihilism I posit the wisdom of contemporary environmental justice, spiritual, and U.S. indigenous thinkers such as Michael Lerner, Vandana Shiva, Cornel West, Marilou Awiakta, Jim Wallis, Joel Kovel, Winona LaDuke, and the late Vine Deloria, Jr. This first chapter ends with the importance of teaching activism to young people, including the need to provide practical training. That theme runs throughout the book, and I draw on concrete examples from my own teaching experience.

Chapter 2, "What David Walker and Harriet Beecher Stowe Still Have to Teach Us," asks what activist writers of the past offer us today. It focuses on the Pequot author and activist William Apess in the early nineteenth century, the black abolitionist David Walker in the 1830s, the famous white abolitionist Harriet Beecher Stowe twenty years later, the well-known nature writer Henry David Thoreau speaking out against slavery then as well, and the African American editor, activist, and author Pauline Hopkins writing at the turn into the twentieth century. All believed passionately in the power of words to generate social change. And they were right. The world could not have looked bleaker to them then than it does to many people now. How could human beings even dream of resisting anti-Indian policies or ending slavery, an institution as old as human history? What could possibly bring an end to the state-sanctioned terrorism of the Ku Klux Klan? This second chapter draws on progressive thinkers today such as Cornel West, Karen Armstrong, James Cone, and Jim Wallis to underline the activist tradition of critique *and* of hope and idealism in representative nineteenth-century texts. These early writers insist on the possibility of radical change, on a new or renewed commitment of people to work to end racial injustice. Two of them, moreover, Thoreau and Hopkins, stand as forebears in the urgent fight we face today for environmental justice and planetary healing.

Chapter 3, "The Multicultural Imperative," focuses on the struggle for racial justice in our own era. It takes issue with the contention that ours is a postrace world (or a postgender, postcolonial, postnational, or postsexuality one). I argue for the continued importance of multiculturalism in the twenty-first century, despite attacks on the concept from both the Right and the Left. Dismissal of multiculturalism impedes both antiracist and environmental justice activism. Multiculturalism can be reduced to nothing more than feel-good diversity, and it has been exploited as a market commodity. Very true. But the answer is not to jettison the concept. The answer lies in reclaiming and redefining multiculturalism as the foundation for social transformation in the postmodern world. This chapter incorporates the thinking of environmental justice activist Vandana Shiva and literary theorist Paula Moya, among others. It also examines the urtext of American racism early in the twentieth century and its continuing impact today, D. W. Griffith's film *The Birth of a Nation* — the KKK recruiting film that launched Hollywood and was the first movie shown in the White House.

Chapter 4, "Rising Waters," shows how ecological issues and the multicultural imperative converge in the passionate call of activist authors today — before it is too late — for environmental justice and planetary healing. Identifying environmental injustices faced by migrant farmworkers, uranium miners, and poor people of color displaced by developers, I concentrate on activist U.S. writers' call right now for a radical shift in belief, a profound realignment of thought and spirit. Novelists Marilynne Robinson and Helena María Viramontes examine the alienating values at the heart of the dominant-culture ethic of conquest and ownership. Gloria Naylor shows that transplanted West African ways of understanding the earth, ways far older than and different from Christianity, offer powerful possibilities for healing in the postmodern world. Simon Ortiz's short stories speak of place-based indigenous truths that all people can embrace if they listen with respect and learn from Native peoples who still remember the sacredness of the creation. These contemporary writers affirm truths voiced by the indigenous and environmental justice thinkers I foreground: Marilou Awiakta, Vine Deloria, Jr., Winona LaDuke, Wendell Berry, and James Cone. A paradigm shift must occur. All human beings must come to understand ourselves as living in relation with — not opposition to or mastery of— the earth and our fellow beings, human and not human.

The last chapter, "Jesus, Marx, and the Future of the Planet," emphasizes that globalization's assault on the planet, people, resources, and all living beings will not stay contained in any one part of the world. That is the message of the two brilliant, contemporary novels by Karen Tei Yamashita and Leslie Marmon Silko with which I end. The consequences of empire always come home. Yamashita and Silko — like Apess, Walker, Stowe, Thoreau, Hopkins, Viramontes, Robinson, Naylor, and Ortiz, all of whom, I stress throughout the book, are simply representative — tell terrible truths. Yamashita shows the devastating attack of global capital on undocumented immigrants and homeless people in the richest nation on earth. Silko provides a terrifying picture of postmodern so-called civilization: torture videos, international trade in body organs, aquifers drained for golf courses, indigenous people incarcerated in their homelands. But Yamashita and Silko, like every writer in this book, also refuse despair and prophesy victory. Each calls for revolution, sometimes literal but always moral and spiritual. Activist U.S. authors, like the progressive thinkers I call particular attention to in this final chapter, Joel Kovel, Vandana Shiva, Vine Deloria, Jr., and Michael Lerner, insist on the power of words to change people and the power of people to change the world.

I argue throughout that the challenge now facing humanists is clear. Inside and outside academic settings we need to revive the liberal arts as a progressive cultural force that not only provides critique but also offers workable ideas and inspiration in the real-world struggle to achieve social justice and restoration of the earth. The activist tradition in American literature, past and present, speaks to that truth.

The question becomes, then, as cultural critics and as cultural artists, how do we generate vision and hope?
—Cornel West, *Prophetic Reflections*

We must change this culture or face extinction.
—Val Plumwood, *Environmental Culture*

# ONE

## Postmodern Fundamentalism

Recently I attended a college graduation ceremony at which three English professors spoke. The first read a long, dark poem about our inability to control life. The second praised the uselessness of studying literature. The third stated that we have the questions, not the answers, and offered an extended interpretation of the final scene of Alfred Hitchcock's *The Birds* as a metaphor for life. Having your eyes pecked out by dive-bombing avians seemed to be the point.

If the new graduates were not terrified of the future and feeling powerless when they marched in, they certainly were when they filed out.

# The Allure of Disdain

It would never do for "art" to be useful.
I don't believe that. What force could be
more powerful than people moving together
with a single voice?
— Wendy Rose, *Bone Dance*

For the past quarter century professional humanists have been theorizing the death of the author and the nonreferentiality of words on the page — the idea that words ("signifiers") refer to nothing actual but, instead, create and produce what we call reality. Meanwhile, right-wing activists in the name of religion bombed abortion clinics, reduced the World Trade Center towers in New York City to cinders, blocked Palestinians' freedom in their own homeland, and promoted a holy war for oil (the president of the United States calling it a "crusade"). People have been killing each other and getting killed because of strong beliefs while elite literary study has by and large been preoccupied with its own inability to believe in anything except critique and the supremacy of irony and irresolvable complexity.

It is not surprising that the prestige of the humanities has declined while "hard" social sciences such as economics and political science have gained stature. As Cornel West observed of poststructuralist literary critics in *Prophetic Reflections* almost two decades ago, "They talk about their subtle relations of rhetoric, knowledge, power, yet they remain silent about *concrete* ways by which people are empowered to resist" (56). Human beings, for good reason, seek answers. Yet for more than twenty-five years the most highly valued academic approach in the humanities has frequently amounted to little more than endless questioning, a process of dismantling certitude upon certitude until all that remains is what I call here postmodern fundamentalism: bedrock commitment to antifoundationalism, indeterminacy, multiplicity, and decenteredness. That is, instability. Nothing to hang on to, nowhere to stand.

In U.S. literary studies this emphasis on the instability of knowledge, the idea that it is socially constructed and therefore we need constantly to question and revise what we know, comes in part from the important activist scholarship and teaching of the 1960s and 1970s. The conservative New Criticism of the 1950s, reflecting cold war isolationism, argued against socially relevant ways of reading. Above all, it believed we should not connect literary study to politics. "New Critics" said readers should concentrate on how the aesthetic properties of a text function in relation to each other, not deal with life outside the text. In disagreement, many young scholars and teachers in the 1960s and 1970s insisted on literature's social relevance. Shaped by the civil rights, antiwar, and women's movements, they argued, as many scholars and teachers do today, that literature encourages multiple interpretations and that political values are always present whether we recognize them or not. As affirmative action opened the doors for people of color and white women such as me to become professors in the last quarter of the twentieth century, feminist, race-based, gay and lesbian, and class-focused critical approaches began to redefine the liberal arts. Such approaches revitalized the humanities inside and outside the academy by demonstrating the crucial role that art and ideas play in the struggle for progressive social change.

At the same time, poststructuralism, often referred to simply as deconstruction, turned away from engagement with social and political issues. Because literature comes to us through words, deconstructionists at prestigious U.S. universities maintained, we need to pursue the question studied by linguist Ferdinand de Saussure and other late nineteenth- and early twentieth-century European theorists: What *are* words? To what do they refer? Anything? How do we know? Before the modern era religion answered those questions in the West. Any culture announcing that in the beginning was the Word ties language to divine purpose and thereby closes debate. But the death of God argued by nineteenth-century Continental philosophers such as Martin Heidegger and Friedrich Nietzsche blasted such confidence. If no God exists, no divine plan for humans or any other life in the universe can be claimed. Meaninglessness rather than meaningfulness defines the modern condition. Human reality consists of exhilarating self-determination, on the one hand, and profound alienation, isolation, and existential loneliness, on the other. Modernity, and now its contemporary offspring, postmodernity, liberates us from repressive authoritarian regimes of knowledge (this is how things are because God or the Bible says so). But it also and terrifyingly cuts us adrift. Is there a knowable purpose to life? No. Is there a divine plan that includes you? No. Each of us is on our own.

In a world lacking any agreed-upon purpose to human life, much less any reliable authority to establish truth, divine or otherwise, why study literature except to ponder our own pain and epistemological distress or escape into diverting linguistic puzzles? The very idea of a literary canon, like the word *canon* itself, reflects a now-irrelevant ecclesiastical mindset. A good deal of feminist, antiracist, sexuality-focused, indigenous, and economically grounded thinking over the last thirty years has resisted this retreat into abstraction. It has continued to stress the importance of literary analysis for activist social change. But poststructuralism, echoing New Criticism's isolationism, maintained that all we can know of what we call reality is our linguistic invention of it. It is fallacious to claim any direct or real relationship between literature and life.

Extremely popular in many U.S. literature departments in the 1980s and 1990s, strict poststructuralist thinking has waned in the twenty-first century. Intense worry about what and whether words mean consumes few humanists today; and even prominent poststructuralists such as Judith Butler now think about the corner that antiuniversalism has backed them into. And many critics — materialist, feminist, race based, multicultural, postcolonial, Native focused, gay rights — never abandoned socially focused ways of reading or commitment to literature's activist role in the world. Nevertheless, there remains a kind of schizophrenia or deep confusion in much literature teaching and scholarship because of the powerful influence that deconstruction had on elite academic thought. Poststructuralism's insistence that we are not talking about anything real in the world when we analyze texts persists as a nagging fear. It often shows up in critics' incredibly complicated, dense prose and use of language. In the early twenty-first century this sometimes takes the form of an avowed — and often quite celebrated — belief in the "inexpressibility" of language, its inability to communicate. It's as if in place of clear meaning, which cannot be produced because it does not exist, lots of difficult, smart-sounding rhetoric can stand in, and maybe no one will notice that little or nothing is said. I recently listened to a bright young scholar give an academic lecture for close to an hour in which she argued for and against reading three novels in terms of identity politics, the idea that one's identity location in the society carries with it political affiliations. Perhaps she was right, but the double move — offering an interpretation and then immediately deconstructing it — has become so predictable that it completely lacked content. All that came through was postmodern paralysis, a reluctance to take any position. Literary criticism has made a fetish of complexity, nuance, and the production of multiple readings for their own sake. Sometimes deconstruction of meaning upon meaning serves knowledge well. But not always.

My point is this. A continuing effect of poststructuralist literary theory has been to make *all* textual meaning complex and unstable, whether it is or not; and frequently this has the convenient apolitical consequence of rendering impossible any clear, defended, activist standpoint. Poststructuralist theory has lured the academy into a postmodern update of New Criticism's view of critical work as an end in itself, literary study as a kind of mammoth brain teaser, the goal of which, in good market-driven fashion, has to do, finally, with nothing more important than individual competition and advancement. Who can produce the subtlest, most nuanced, or surprising analysis? Generating erudite readings based on close, clever, tightly focused examinations of specific arrangements of words on the page (precisely what was taught in the 1950s) has returned par excellence as the job of the literary critic, right down to revival of "close reading" as the announced task at hand. In the early 1980s Raymond Williams warned:

> There is a kind of attachment to specificity and complexity which
> is the condition of any adequate intellectual work, and another
> kind which is really a defence of a particular kind of consciousness.
> ... Thus we have always to distinguish between two kinds of
> consciousness: that alert, open and usually troubled recognition
> of specificity and complexity, which is always, in a thousand instances, putting working generalizations and hypotheses under

strain; and that other, often banal, satisfaction with specificity and complexity, as reasons for the endless postponement of all (even local) general judgements or decisions. (181–82)

Ambiguity and multiplicity have become ends in themselves in much liberal arts scholarship and teaching, which should not be surprising. Many academic humanists inhabit an intellectual context unsure about or even openly hostile to the idea of universal truths. Indeterminacy is the highest value that postmodernism as a worldview can offer.

RELIGIOUS FUNDAMENTALISM, only a century or so old, as scholars such as Karen Armstrong explain, fears that secular thinking has as its goal the wiping out of religion, which is largely true, of course. In response, religious fundamentalism digs in. It insists on the literal veracity of its belief system: the declared truths revealed in its sacred texts, whether the Torah, the Bible, the Qur'an, or the Book of Mormon. From the point of view of the religious fundamentalist, to question those declared truths is to render oneself an apostate, a person outside the fold, hopelessly fallen from the group.

While the secular academy disdains such literalism and blind allegiance to authority, as it should, it simultaneously and ironically practices its own parallel and no less mindless orthodoxy in its adherence to postmodernism as a faith system. So familiar by now that it is part of the cultural air we breathe in the modern West, postmodernism as a belief system has both dogma and creed. It worships antifoundationalism (there is no first principle or knowable foundation for knowledge or belief), relativism (there are no absolutes), self-reflexivity (without absolutes you are all that you can know, if that), decenteredness (without any first principle or absolutes there can be no center), and instability (all is dispersal and flux). A weakened belief in history plus an emphasis on surface as all that exists, as much postmodern visual art and architecture make obvious, flow logically from this worldview. Perhaps most important, postmodern fundamentalism's most admired affective and intellectual behaviors consist of irony, cynicism, and despair. In a universe without center, foundation, meaning, or purpose, what other responses could possibly make sense?

If these values affected only the thinking of academics, ordinary people could care less. But postmodern thought saturates the contemporary world. The values theorized in the academy parallel the felt reality of millions. Life in the developed world is characterized by acute feelings of disconnect between people. Around the world and across all economic classes, loss of direction and an absence of hope run rampant among huge numbers of young people in particular. For many of them, meaningful life's work, which represents a very natural wish, seems less and less possible even to imagine, much less achieve, especially in a global economy experiencing serial collapse. Belief in moral absolutes finds almost no broad-based expression in the United States, where shopping and overconsumption seem to be the highest goods. Should we be surprised that cynicism, stemming from feelings of powerlessness and purposelessness, frequently dominates public thought, especially among the young?

Certainly, there are many humanists who continue to advocate socially committed value systems such as feminism, egalitarianism, ecocentrism, Native sovereignty, and socialism. They have, from the 1960s on, insisted on the meaning and purpose of progressive struggle. Others respond by advocating pragmatism. They concede the meaninglessness of the universe but argue that we need to proceed as if meaning and universals exist. Really smart intellectuals, however, reject such thinking. They know the only rational, sophisticated response to postmodern reality is to own the brutal truth of nihilism. Failure to do so doesn't make you a sinner, religious fundamentalism's worst category, but a fool, postmodern fundamentalism's. In other words, and I am certainly not the first to say this, for all its antifoundationalism, antiessentialism, relativism, and decenteredness, postmodernism is at core essentialist. Its essentialism consists not of God but of its own supreme principle, which is simply the flip side of religious fundamentalism's: the insistence that there is no spiritual reality.

It makes perfect sense that insecurity grips the liberal arts and the study of literature in particular. Even as many professional humanists talk about social injustice, wish for progressive change, and passionately critique systems of power that oppress people, they practice a knee-jerk adherence to the fundamentalist dogma of postmodernism. Everything is complex, nothing simple. There are no universals, only socially constructed and highly temporal and historically shifting patterns of belief. There is no right or wrong, only culturally invented versions of both, and no truth, only multiple and constantly shifting "truth claims." There is no center, no transcendence, no knowledge except that gained through reason, which can and always must be deconstructed. This is the postmodern fundamentalism that the humanities too often teach the young, a faith system of nihilism and powerlessness that many professional humanists bravely model, preach, catechize. And if young people are really smart and buy what we are selling, we reward them by accepting them into graduate school and inducting them as future practitioners.

## The Crisis in the Humanities

Most of us have learned to accommodate to a world that has been flattened, made one-dimensional, disenchanted, despiritualized. And yet, we feel an abiding hunger because human beings are theotropic — they turn toward the sacred — and that dimension in us cannot be fully extinguished.
— Michael Lerner, *The Left Hand of God*

Several decades of fierce debate about the proper role of the humanities are now largely over. While some remain avid social activists and others strict deconstructionists, most professional humanists fall somewhere in between, eclectically mixing bits and pieces of Marxism, feminism, and antiracism, for instance, with bits and pieces of poststructuralist theory. This stir enables production of endless critiques of power relations without any actual political engagement — this is the eclectic first half: critique without activism — because poststructuralism undermines the idea that either words or actions matter. Put another way, progressive academic postmodernity encourages humanists to be rigorous, even brilliant, social critics who are simultaneously cynical, detached, always questioning and disbelieving, and above all suspicious or even contemptuous of anything that looks like faith, conviction, earnestness, or hope. Those are not only ridiculously irrational but also — cardinal sin in the academy — stupid.

What this means is that in the United States the fundamentalist Christian Right and the liberal postmodernist Left often agree. Explicitly or implicitly, both preach that human agency is impotent, earthly disaster is inevitable, and the future is out of our control. For fundamentalist Christians, this is good news. Because only God has power, the end of human life on earth, the "rapture," at which point the saved will ascend to live eternally in heaven and all others will be consigned to eternal damnation, is to be welcomed. There is no point working on this world because it will soon end. Indeed, the worse things get, the better. Destruction of life on earth presages realization of the divine plan, arrival of the Judgment Day.

For the postmodernist Left, human agency is also pointless, not because God or some other first principle (there is none) is busy plotting the end of life on earth but because human agency is an illusion. We cannot create a better world. Old-fashioned liberal thinking believed we could, but it was naively attached to flawed Enlightenment thinking. It subscribed to the idea that life has meaning, human progress is possible, and we can transform the world if we attempt to. From a postmodernist point of view, the history of the human race and reason prove such thinking delusional. Nihilism represents the only logical posture to assume in a meaningless universe over which we have no control. There is no point working on this world because it is irrational — in fact, crazy — to believe it makes a difference to do so.

The equation works the same in either case. For Christian fundamentalists, activism in the service of social justice in this world runs counter to the divine plan. For postmodern fundamentalists, activism in the service of social justice in this world runs counter to reason. The first group may find delight in letting the world go to hell in a handcart, and the second sadness, even desolation. But go we will. In each case elders teach the young to see what is wrong in the world humans have made and then to believe it is either sinful or impossible to do anything about it.

Of course, most progressive humanists do not take pleasure in offering hopelessness to the young. Often we do not even recognize that is what we are doing. Rather, we are simply doing our job when we pile depressing critical analysis upon depressing critical analysis. Our task is to open young people's eyes to oppressive systems of human power, how they work, and how we are all involved in them. We expose the injustices and the ideologies driving them. Many of us focus especially on the time period since the Renaissance, which has witnessed increasingly disastrous Western global dominance, for this is the era in which we still live. We help others see the importance of interrogating the bases of contemporary thought in order to understand destructive forces in the world today such as racism, environmental devastation, and economic imperialism.

This is enormously important work, as people outside and inside academic settings recognize. Unless we identify what is wrong, we cannot heal the grievous wounds that human beings inflict on each other and the earth.

But that is the issue I am raising: the *purpose* of professional humanists' analyses and critiques. If they are not in the service of positive social change, why do they exist? If we do not include answers alongside critiques, hope alongside anger, and activism alongside discourse and *talk about both terms* in each of these pairs, what is the point? We simply become the twenty-first century's proverbial monks in an ivory tower counting the number of angels on the head of a pin, as I believe more and more people suspect has become the case. I think of my sister who spent years directing an urban child care center or my other sister who taught nursing. I think of my neighbor who organizes workers in the local service employees' union or the young man down the block who dropped out of high school and now wonders what to do with his life. I have in mind the parent of a young person hoping to chart a future that is socially meaningful or a retired person considering how to use her energy. Thousands — millions — of thoughtful people wish to make a positive contribution to progressive social change and restoration of the planet. The liberal arts should be offering practical, useful inspiration to everyone seeking to create a different and better world.

At every level, starting with elementary education, funding and respect for the arts and humanities have diminished greatly in the United States over the last three decades. I have heard colleagues at various institutions complain that the seriousness of college students taking humanities courses has dropped. Young people major in the natural and hard social sciences or engineering, business, and other vocational areas and then sign up for literature, history, philosophy, religion, film, or art history classes to enjoy themselves. In part, this reflects economics. Annette Kolodny quite correctly points out in *Academe* that students and their parents need postsecondary education to prepare graduates to make money. The cost of college forces them to be practical. But the truth is, the average business major is no more certain to walk out of college into a job in the early twenty-first century than the average English major. Yet one is perceived as the source of a useful body of knowledge for life and work in the world, and the other is not. That perception ought to concern all progressive people, including and above all humanists themselves, both inside and outside academic settings. The liberal arts are in decline in the U.S. education system and in the culture at large for economic reasons. But it may also be that professional humanists have lost their way and need to rethink and then clearly communicate the purpose of the liberal arts.

THE VAUNTED PURPOSE of the humanities as I write is "critical thinking." That is the mantra of academic administrations and professional humanists themselves. We exist to analyze and critique cultural material: print, visual, historical, contemporary. I agree. But *why*? That is the question. Endlessly analyzing and critiquing without belief that we can and must as human beings create significant change becomes, after a point, an exercise in masochism. Since most people, happily, are not masochists, they, unhappily, come to regard the humanities as interesting but finally not the place where they gain useful, practical knowledge beyond the private and personal. The liberal arts as a place to learn not only what's wrong in the world but also *how we might fix it* — what actions, personal and collective, we might take to change the world for the better — needs to become the goal. In the past, as Russell A. Berman points out and believes should once again be the case, the humanities and especially the study of literature represented an important site for exploring the questions, How should we live our lives? What ethical values should guide us? I agree but push the point further. The liberal arts need to go beyond the personal and individualistic to include the question of group activism: what can and should *we do* in order to advance progressive social change?

The tremendous value of the humanities and especially of the study of literature resides in the power of texts to teach us about ourselves, individually and corporately, including the systems of injustice that we as human beings create. But the value of the humanities also resides in the power of words to inspire us, to transform us, to give us strength and courage for the difficult task of *re*-creating the world. That is an outrageously out-of-step, unpostmodern idea — as became obvious in the widespread euphoria about "change" in the United States following the 2008 presidential election. It is, however, the real reason most people who find meaning in the humanities do so. We pay lip service to postmodern fundamentalism, but, in fact, most of us believe texts *do* contain truths — even Truth — that we ardently want others, especially young people, to see. Many professional humanists do an excellent job of foregrounding negatives, whether they consist of explicit themes, such as Hawthorne's attack on Christian hypocrisy in *The Scarlet Letter*, or show up more subliminally, such as that same novel's anti-Indian racism despite its claim to be concerned about injustice. What we do not do nearly as well is bring to the surface and talk seriously about the hope and idealism that drive our own critical acts and that structure most of the texts we choose to deal with.

Animating the fiercely critical American literature I typically teach and write about, books such as *Uncle Tom's Cabin, The Souls of Black Folk*, and *Almanac of the Dead*, is fury that things are not as they should be but also a call, implicit or explicit, to *do something about it*. Not disdain and despair but hope and a call to action — belief that things are wrong *and people have the power to change them* — define much of the American literary tradition. That tradition contains contradictions. It is not perfect. But that fact does not destroy its value.

Progressive humanists need to remain rigorous, honest, and unafraid in their analyses. But we also need to become more visionary and activist. If the liberal arts are only about deconstructing, exposing the problems and modeling skepticism, irony, and critique-as-an-end-in-itself, *without any attention to answers, hope, and activism*, then what are we doing except, to recall Audre Lorde's famous metaphor, attempting to dismantle the master's house using the master's tools? In fact, I fear we aren't dismantling anything, despite all the pride in deconstruction. I think we are actually *building* the master's house, constructing an edifice of despair that renovates the very structures of oppression that our critical analyses work so hard to lay bare. When erudite humanists argue, whether directly or indirectly, that words do not attach meaningfully to material reality, elegant ironic detachment is the ultimate goal of intelligent people, and real social change will never happen, they do, I am saying, the work of the system for it.

IN *ETHICS AFTER IDEALISM* Rey Chow thinks about poststructuralism from the point of view of cultural studies, which stresses the importance of class and race as material and political realities. Chow notes how poststructuralist theory, positioning itself within the academy as subversive and radical when it first appeared, actually reinforced the status quo:

> For all its fundamental epistemological subversiveness, the dislocation of the sign as philosophized in the heyday of "high theory" could still be contained within a more or less European tradition. One could, for instance, trace the work of Derrida back to Lévi-Strauss, Saussure, Husserl, Heidegger, Nietzsche, and ultimately to Kant. This explains why, for nearly two decades in North America, an act as avant-garde and as radical as dislocating the sign was paradoxically practiced in the most elitist educational institutions, such as Yale, Johns Hopkins, and Cornell, where the followers of deconstruction enjoyed the best of both spiritual and material worlds, as mental radicals and as well-paid Ivy League professors. (4–5)

As Chow reminds us, the first thinkers in the United States to embrace the new critical orthodoxy of poststructuralism were powerful white men at powerful white institutions writing and teaching at a time when feminist, race-based, and economically focused perspectives were unsettling the academy by challenging both the ideas and the human makeup of those institutions.

Poststructuralism's convenient reassertion of white masculine intellectual authority has always been obvious to some. Most famous, perhaps, is black feminist scholar Barbara Christian's essay "The Race for Theory," which charged as early as 1987 that the infatuation with high

European theory represented a return to business as usual. In *Learning from Experience* Paula Moya ponders the motives of poststructuralist critics today who attack the validity of identity politics as a standpoint: "A generous reading demands that we take postmodernist critics at their word, and that we accept the idea that they believe that all but the most strategic claims to identity are essentialist and therefore politically pernicious. A less generous reading, but one that also deserves consideration, is that the charge of essentialism might also result from a racist counterstance to the agency of newly politicized minorities" (9). As Moya, Christian, and numerous others wonder, how accidental can it be that just when feminist and race-based scholarship challenges the ultramale, ultrawhite composition of the academic canon and the professoriate, high theory solves the problem by announcing the death of the author and the irrelevance of identity categories?

Moya's *Learning from Experience* and Satya P. Mohanty's *Literary Theory and the Claims of History* defend identity politics in a postmodern context by turning to what is known as postpositive realism. As Moya explains, contemporary philosophical realism allows us to understand identity and experience in ways that avoid the simple empiricism of the past, on the one hand, and postmodernism's radical anti-essentialism, on the other. Postpositive realism argues that it is possible to arrive at objective truth based on analysis and observation, that is, on our experience. Such knowledge is not absolutist but always subject to revision, much as science makes claims always subject to revision. But this does mean we can talk about universals such as "the good" and structure our lives accordingly as long as, again, we remain constantly open to the possibility of revision.

This concept of objective knowledge is not dogmatic, rigid, fixed. Rather, it says that our knowledge is always in process: a seeking for truth that arrives at truths contingently and in a spirit of willingness to revise if reason and experience dictate. But it does say there is ground to stand on in the postmodern world. We can talk about truth, truths, normative values, identity politics, and human agency without falling into the absolutism of either fundamentalism, the religious one on the far right, which tells us what to believe, or the secular one on the far left, which tells us belief is dead.

The path laid out by Moya and Mohanty resembles what many spiritual teachers have always known. We are fallible. We can only seek truth. We can never achieve perfect knowledge. But we can know imperfectly, and we can and must seek. That is what it means to be human.

## Belief

The mystery of it all, though, has taught me that whatever is sought by wise men and women must be approached through Art.
— Elizabeth Cook-Lynn, *Notebooks*

If you were in a coma from the mid-1980s to the end of the first decade of the twenty-first century, you missed the fact that religious belief — faith in something greater than oneself — dominated world politics. Otherwise, you know that for a number of years U.S. elections depended on which candidate secured right-wing fundamentalist Christian support, wars erupted and martyrs emerged because of ideological spiritual differences, and families divided along born-again/damned fault lines. My own personal favorite occurred when my nephew described in great detail how I was going to burn in hell for all eternity. All I could think was that I had already arrived as we sat crammed among family members in the backseat of an un-air-conditioned car speeding along a rural Ohio state route in 102-degree heat.

Many progressive people that I know consider religion bad or stupid: a superstitious hangover from the past, the mark of a conventional or timid mind, and the cause of far more evil and oppression in the world than good or enlightenment. In many ways I agree. But as liberal scholar, activist, and rabbi Michael Lerner points out, this dismissal demands reconsideration. While the Left has been heaping contempt on religion, the pews of evangelical churches have been filling. It behooves those of us not there to ask what those religious communities offer people. Why do they go? Obvious answers declare that religious people crave something to believe in, they wish to stave off meaninglessness and the existential isolation of postmodern life, they yearn for some sense of community and human connection, they seek continuity with past and future generations. All of this, Lerner explains, is not to be mocked but taken seriously and reflected upon. For those are the desires of all of us.

WE ARE SPIRITUAL as well as physical, intellectual, and emotional beings. That is understood by all of the activist progressive thinkers I rely on in this book — Lerner, Cornel West, Jim Wallis, Marilou Awiakta, Vine Deloria, Jr., Winona LaDuke, James H. Cone, Joel Kovel, Vandana Shiva. Human beings seek meaning, transcendent values larger than ourselves that call us together in common cause and shared community. Lerner observes of the secular Left's horror of the religious Right:

> Many secularists imagine that people drawn to the Right are there solely because of some ethical or psychological malfunction. What they miss is that there are many very decent Americans who get attracted to the Religious Right because it is the only voice that they

encounter that is willing to challenge the despiritualization of daily life, to call for a life that is driven by higher purpose than money, and to provide actual experiences of supportive community for those whose daily life is suffused with alienation and spiritual loneliness. (3)

The solution for Lerner lies in the Left, both secular and religious, owning the spirituality of its own progressive politics: not pretending to an aspiritual politics but, instead, defining and claiming the transcendent ethical values on which leftist political agendas are based. All politics, he emphasizes, is about values, many if not all of them deriving from beliefs also expressed in various religious teachings about how to treat one another, ourselves, our fellow beings on the planet, and the planet itself. Politics, like religion, is about belief. The Right admits and exploits this. The Left, Lerner argues, instead of renouncing any and all overlap of religion and politics, needs to foreground its own politics of meaning, what he calls its own spiritual politics. The phrase does not designate a doctrinal or creed-specific politics. It refers to a leftist politics that advocates its own values as not simply socially good but also morally — across a broad range of spirituality — right.

I invoke Lerner here because he has the courage as a liberal activist to call the secular Left to account for its arrogance. How pleasant (read: narcissistic) to believe that everyone on the right is a fool, that everyone who feels born-again has been duped, that everyone who believes in and seeks the sacred in daily life is caught in a time warp. Lerner's caution against dismissing those who believe in faith-based social transformation as naive inferior thinkers is one that all humanists should reflect on, not because we should all become religious people (that is not Lerner's point either) but because many of us, whether we admit it or not, are drawn to the humanities because we are, in fact, deeply motivated by faith ourselves: our hope for progressive social transformation.

I also invoke Lerner to underline a parallel. Just as he believes the political Left loses people to the religious Right when it focuses on attacking faith-based values instead of owning its own liberal ones, I think the humanities are losing power inside and outside academic institutions because humanists focus almost entirely on denying the existence of transcendent values instead of owning the progressive ones that inform the vision of most of us. Many people in the United States crave a liberal politics of meaning, as Lerner puts it. So too, I believe, many people in the United States, including in our secondary and postsecondary school classrooms as well as throughout society, crave a reclamation of the culture from the postmodern nihilism into which it has too often descended. I think many wish for a revival of the humanities as a progressive cultural force capable not simply of providing critique but also of offering hope and inspiration in the real-world activist struggle for social justice.

Cornel West, for instance, who is also (as many tend to forget) a lay preacher, thinks seriously about what social scientists Pearl and Samuel Oliner explain has been described as the modern "malaise of the soul" (1). In *Prophetic Reflections* West reflects on the "nihilism and cynicism" that he sees "especially among the working poor and very poor in the United States" (52) and observes: "Our culture of consumption says that one finds meaning through possessions. And in the black community there is a particularly acute spiritual crisis of meaning" (78). He cites the important influence on him of Marx plus an impressive range of postmodernist scholars who teach us deep ways of understanding how power works. Yet his own "left Christianity," he emphasizes, is "in part a response to those dimensions of life that have been flattened out, to the surface-like character of a postmodern culture that refuses to speak to issues of despair, that refuses to speak to issues of the absurd" (91). Asked about erudite theoretical arguments that we cannot know or speak of the real in our era of hyperreality, West replies: "To be an upper-middle-class American is actually to live a life of unimaginable comfort, convenience, and luxury. Half of the black population is denied this, which is why they have a strong sense of reality" (91). West's refusal to romanticize postmodern nihilism by adopting its postures or limiting its disastrous spiritual effects to people with privilege models an important ethical stance in the contemporary world.

Joining West and Lerner, white Christian evangelical preacher and progressive activist Jim Wallis argues in *The Soul of Politics* that the crisis we now face is "one of the spirit — deeper than just the turns and twists of secular politics" (39). Unfamiliar perhaps to many academic humanists who frequently (and erroneously) equate evangelicalism and fundamentalism, Wallis in several books as well as the journal he edits, *Sojourners*, and his life spent living and ministering among homeless people in Washington, D.C., articulates a liberal vision of social transformation in the United States. It is grounded in Christian teachings and committed to antiracism, antisexism, the elimination of poverty, replacement of the dominant-culture ethic of earth mastery with one of relationship, and healing of our addiction to consumption. Hailing a "prophetic spirituality" (45), he is unabashed in his belief that "historically, religion has been a source of guidance for spiritual and moral values. Transcendence calls us to accountability and gives us a sense of meaning and purpose we are unable to find on our own. Without ethics rooted in transcendent reality, moral sensibility becomes merely a matter of shifting cultural consensus" (49). Owning spiritual faith as a source for progressive struggle, Wallis rejects the logic of postmodern indeterminacy, epistemological uncertainty, and the absence of universals.

Lerner, West, and Wallis refuse to offer only critique. Social criticism without belief in our ability to create change and activist commitment to do so only aggrandizes the critic, demonstrating his or her brilliance. It does nothing to alter the situation. Addressing such paralysis, Wallis ends his best-selling book *God's Politics: Why the Right Gets It Wrong and the Left Doesn't Get It* by quoting a fellow activist, Lisa Sullivan, who would routinely respond to laments that the world needs a new Martin Luther King, Jr., by angrily insisting: "We are the ones we have been waiting for!" Wallis agrees. Change will come from "people who, because of faith and hope, believe that the world can be changed. And it is that very belief that changes the world. And if not us, who will believe? After all, we are the ones we have been waiting for" (374). Significantly, at least from my point of view, this clear affirmation of belief in the power of human agency in this life and the imperative of activist progressive social change comes not from the halls of academe but from an evangelical Christian minister who, though a best-selling author and regular guest on National Public Radio, enjoys little if any respect as a thinker among elite professional humanists.

NOT EVERYONE needs to be religious. Nor is religion in and of itself a good thing. History and contemporary events demonstrate the terrible effects that religious thought and practices can and have had at every level of human life, as passionate arguments by atheists such as Richard Dawkins and Christopher Hitchens reveal. Neither is it the case that religion, much less Judaism or Christianity, represents the only repository of faith-based transformative values. Other bodies of thought are also capable of guiding and inspiring us as human beings to live with and on the earth in peace and to work for and achieve social justice. Marxism, as many artists and writers and much modern history testify, is a crucially important, secular, faith-based visionary system of values that can inspire fundamental, progressive change. Likewise, deep ethical commitment to secular values of egalitarianism and ecocentrism can constitute an empowering faith standpoint capable of leading society to profound, positive change. Above all, Native American worldviews, as I will emphasize repeatedly, offer crucial wisdom and a clear path to much-needed radical moral revolution in the contemporary world.

Many more humanists today, rather than scoffing at spiritual belief and rejecting utopian ideas, need to reengage both. We need to support the visionary project of progressive social transformation and foreground the urgency of planetary restoration by emphasizing the values and actions that enable both. Too much literary endeavor in particular, in my view, has given up on or ignores that broad activist mission. It tends to replace vision with endlessly repetitious intellectual mastery of a tiny set of erudite Western thinkers such as Freud, Lacan, Derrida, Kant. Or it gets stuck in close reading, critique, and critical thinking as pleasurable (perhaps) but finally pointless ends in themselves.

Progressive U.S. religious thinkers, including Lerner, West, Wallis, and black liberation theologians James H. Cone and Katie Geneva Cannon, offer liberal humanists a number of things. First, they remind us that, regardless of one's personal choices, religious belief remains extremely important in the United States. To ignore the subject entirely or heap contempt on it severely limits the audience liberal humanists reach. A 2008 Pew Forum survey found that 71 percent of Americans consider their belief in God or a universal spirit absolutely certain, with another 17 percent fairly certain. For 58 percent of those surveyed, religion plays a very important role in their life, with another 25 percent judging it somewhat important. Interestingly, the survey found these believers more tolerant in outlook than might be assumed of such a faith-professing nation. Many religions can lead to eternal life, 70 percent said, and 68 percent agreed that more than one way of interpreting their own religious teachings exists. Second, contemporary liberal religious thought can help illuminate literature written from openly religious perspectives, as I will turn to in the next chapter especially. But third and most important, this body of thought, along with various secular systems of ethics and much Native American thinking, calls explicit and unapologetic attention to the widespread human need for belief, hope, transcendent values, purpose larger than oneself, and dedication to shared, corporate action for the social good. Progressive humanists can and should be speaking boldly to these needs.

It's not a matter of humanists infusing their thinking with specific religious doctrines or agendas; and I am especially and adamantly aware of the disastrous impacts that Abrahamic fundamentalisms such as right-wing fundamentalist Christianity have had and continue to have globally. Environmental justice scholar and activist Vandana Shiva accurately points in *Earth Democracy* to the shared patriarchal values of unregulated capitalism and contemporary Western religion. She says that we have now with globalization "not a contest between, but a convergence of, religious and capitalist patriarchy in the form of religious fundamentalism and market fundamentalism" (132). Shiva believes religion could be "a countervailing value system to the excesses of the market" (133) but is not. Lerner, West, Wallis, Cone, and Cannon concur, which is why they critique the same global injustices and desecration of the planet decried by Shiva and distance themselves from right-wing fundamentalism as fiercely as she.

Motivating the powerful environmental justice activism of Shiva, who lives and works in India, are this-world anger and hope, the first righteous and the second transcendent. She despises the systems of human greed and oppression that ravage the earth and target huge numbers of the world's poor, most of whom are people of color, especially women and children. But she has faith in human beings. She expresses deep hope that because humans have created these systems we can and will recognize their fundamental immorality and take collective action to change them.

Likewise not avowing religious belief but also not mired in postmodernist angst or academic debates about what is real, Marxist Joel Kovel maintains that there are such things as truth, efficacious action, and hope: "If truth gives clarity and definition to our world, if it weans us from dependency on alienating forces that sap our will and delude our mind, and if it can bring us together with others in a common empowering project — a project that gives us hope that we can become the makers of our own history — why, then, then it makes us free even if what it reveals is terrible to behold" (vii). Kovel states bluntly: "Refusal is worthless unless coupled with affirmation" (xv). Critique without belief that we can know what is true and can act on that basis means nothing.

Progressive humanists need to admit that the emperor has no clothes. The stakes are too high for academicians to continue wondering whether signifiers have referents or the author is dead or alive. The stakes are too high for liberal people in general to debate whether life has meaning or not. As I write, the planet is heating, human beings are being forced to sell their own body organs to survive, species are being extinguished, obese children in rich parts of the world are developing diabetes while poor children elsewhere starve, multinational corporations are patenting life forms and selling water, and nuclear weapons will soon orbit the earth. One response is to see, critique, and rue these problems and then hide out in close readings of texts and elegant nihilism or, outside the academy, despair and denial. The other, modeled by West, Lerner, Wallis, Cone, Cannon, Shiva, Kovel, and many others but none more than indigenous thinkers and activists, is to insist on the following. There are truths, and we do know what they are. Hope exists, and it is not an option to retreat into despair. The earth is alive and sacred, and we human beings are part of the creation, not masters of it. We can and must make changes so that we live together in ways that respect the planet, each other, all living beings, and the creative first principle, however we name or conceptualize that reality.

INDIGENOUS THINKERS in the United States emphasize that the spiritual crisis in postmodern America is endemic to Western civilization itself. Cynicism and nihilism — contempt for the sacred and a profound disregard for the creation — have defined Western thought and behavior for centuries. Winona LaDuke explains in *Recovering the Sacred* that "Native spiritual practices and Judeo-Christian traditions are based on very different paradigms" (12), with the earth viewed as a subject, not an object, in Native worldviews, which are place based and regard human beings as part of the creation. LaDuke emphasizes that indigenous societies are "built on those spiritual foundations — the relationship of peoples to their sacred lands, to relatives with fins or hooves, to the plant and animal foods that anchor a way of life" (12). When it was first published more than three decades ago, Vine Deloria's *God Is Red* foresaw the modern Western world's "imminent and expected destruction of the life cycle of world ecology." Deloria warned then and reiterates in the book's reissue in the twenty-first century that only a fundamental shift in values can reverse this disastrous course — a "shift in viewpoint [that] is essentially religious, not economic or political" (288). The spiritual crisis that racks postmodern civilization, Deloria, LaDuke, and numerous indigenous thinkers have explained over and over again, has deep roots. Native leaders in what is now the United States have from first contact told white people that they must change how they see the creation and themselves if human beings are to survive.

Linda Hogan expresses hope that Native and non-Native people can come together in understanding that the earth is alive and not to be desecrated. She states: "It is clear that we have strayed from the treaties we once had with the land and with the animals. It is also clear, and heartening, that in our time there are many — Indian and non-Indian alike — who want to restore and honor these broken agreements" (11). But major change depends on dominant Western values undergoing radical reorientation, Hogan's reflections make obvious. As she observes, there is a "spiritual fragmentation that has accompanied our ecological destruction" (52). A culture that condones the torture of animals to satisfy the curiosity of researchers or needs to conduct experiments to learn if animals communicate or can remember pain and trauma is fundamentally estranged from the creation.

Cherokee/Appalachian writer and activist Marilou Awiakta tells how the Cherokee chief Attakullakulla, meeting with whites to negotiate a treaty, looked around in surprise. "Where are your women?" he asked. The prospect of men alone making decisions was alarming. It suggested a basic cultural and spiritual dysfunction. "To the Cherokee," Awiakta says, "reverence for women/Mother Earth/life/spirit is interconnected. Irreverence for one is likely to mean irreverence for all.

Implicit in their chief's question, 'Where are your women?' the Cherokee hear, 'Where is your balance? What is your intent?' They see that balance is absent and are wary of the white men's motives. They intuit the mentality of destruction" (92). Awiakta stresses that liberation from that mentality into a different and life-supporting ethic has never been more urgent.

THE QUESTION OF human survival is finally not scientific or technological but moral and spiritual. Will human beings schooled in destructive paradigms of dominance and subordination have the courage and wisdom to reorient our values and beliefs so that we affirm and respect life on earth, and, if we make that choice, will we act to create progressive change? That question needs to guide and shape our vision as humanists. It is grounded in certain absolutes, among them the facts that human beings need meaning and that some values such as respect for the planet and life on it are universal and unchanging. Michael Lerner is right when he says that there is in the United States a "spiritual crisis that the most visible forces of the Left have been unable to address, largely because they don't even recognize spiritual needs as a central reality of contemporary life" (44). Humanists in general need to reengage rather than reject spiritual issues. Academic humanists in particular need to question the origins and purpose of their obsession with negativity, their practice of critique for its own sake, and, too often, their contempt for hope and activism. These have become the new postmodern orthodoxy, the new secular fundamentalist faith in nihilism that, like all fundamentalisms, limits rather than enables progressive change.

## Pedagogy

Heightening students' awareness of racism without also developing an
awareness of the possibility of change is a prescription for despair.
— Beverly Daniel Tatum, "Talking about Race, Learning about Racism"

In a lecture for fellow academics in 2007 a young scholar of American
literature gave an impressive account of her teaching and research in
which she repeated a number of times how depressing her students find
most of the reading in her course on twentieth-century U.S. literature
because the writers so often focus on poverty, sexism, and racism. The
young faculty member ended her presentation by stressing the importance of giving students hope. During the question-and-answer period
an audience member asked how she does that. In response she invoked
famous theorists — Foucault, Bhabha, Bakhtin — to explain her belief
that we teach students well how to analyze issues and recognize resistance in literature. But she admitted that she did not know how to give
students hope. She paused and added: "I do not know what to tell them
to place their hope in."

This question of hope — essentially a spiritual question, a question
of belief — is one humanists must be able to answer if we hope to oc-
cupy more than a minor role in the twenty-first century, in or out of
the academy. In particular, professional humanists must answer the
question, and soon, or it will almost certainly be answered in ways that
destroy the last half century of progressive scholarship and teaching.
In 2009, as Matt Sedensky reports, Tullian Tchividjian, grandson of
Billy Graham, became the newly elected leader of a powerful, arch-
conservative, U.S. megachurch with a worldwide radio and TV audience. Tchividjian had this to say of his ministry: "I think that politics is
one strategic area of cultural engagement. . . . But I also think that the

sphere of art and the sphere of education and the sphere of media and technology are also strategic." Religious fundamentalism will not confine itself to politics. The arts and education, along with popular media, Tchividjian emphasizes, represent the logical, exciting, next frontier.

In *Education's End: Why Our Colleges and Universities Have Given Up on the Meaning of Life*, Yale law professor Anthony Kronman correctly observes: "While emphasizing the importance of questions of meaning and purpose that transcend the narrowly vocational, few liberal arts programs today provide a place for their sustained and structured exploration" (41). Kronman points out that in the contemporary academic research climate humanists no longer believe they can or should provide answers. "They insist that they are not professionally qualified to lead their students in the search for an answer to the question of what living is for. The subject may of course come up outside of class, where teacher and student feel free to speak in more intimate terms. But few college or university teachers today believe they have either the right or duty to offer their students organized instruction in the value and purpose of living" (42). Kronman's solution, however, is to turn back the clock. The value and purpose of life are for him intensely personal questions, the answers to which he finds in the great texts of Western civilization. The enemy of that tradition he identifies as "political correctness," defined by him as the confluence of diversity, multiculturalism, and constructivism. To regain direction and status, the humanities in his view need to return to the classics, in his presentation an overwhelmingly white male canon. He regards the complexion of that tradition as incidental, for the great books are timeless and transcendent.

At the other end of the spectrum, Stanley Fish extols humanities education that is hermetically sealed off from engagement with current events and refuses to take any position on issues of the day. Do politics belong in the classroom? Absolutely not. "I adhere to the distinction between pedagogy and political advocacy, and I do so effortlessly. . . . It never even occurs to me to turn the discussion into an occasion for pronouncing on the political questions of the day, and because the parameters of the discussion are so clearly set and so clearly academic, my students know better than to introduce such questions. Set it up right and you won't go wrong." And when people ask why liberal arts professors do what they do? "The demand for justification, as I have said in other places, always come[s] from those outside the enterprise. Those inside the enterprise should resist it, because to justify something is to diminish it by implying its value lies elsewhere. If the question *What justifies what you do?* won't go away, the best answer to give is 'nothing.'" Now that should do it. Just ridicule the question and, poof, the issue will disappear.

IF ACADEMIC HUMANISTS do not want to concede the question of values and purpose to Kronman's great white masters, much less to right-wing religious fundamentalists, or give up on relevance altogether with Fish, or continue directionless and without purpose except to read texts closely and point out all that is wrong in the world, we had better address the issues of hope and purpose head-on for ourselves. First, we need to link our work to the progressive antiracist, feminist, materialist, gay and lesbian, and anti-imperialist work of the last half century. Then, we need to insist on activism in the service of positive change as part of our mission. Liberal arts faculty need to own the fact that there *is* real-world purpose to our teaching. We wish to see acted upon in the world the ideals of equity and justice that liberal humanities study advocates. This includes analytical attention to oppression and injustice, which we do well. It also includes attention to the questions of hope and action, which we do not do well.

The young crave such teaching. As Paolo Freire says of all genuine education, "We study, we learn, we teach, we know with our entire body. We do all of these things with feeling, with emotion, with wishes, with fear, with doubts, with passion, and also with critical reasoning. However, we never study, learn, teach, or know with the last only" (xxv). Unless evacuated of all connection to our lives, humanities study stirs up powerful feelings. It raises profound and often upsetting questions about the meaning of life, the social systems invented by human beings, our treatment of ourselves and each other, and our relationship to all other living beings and to the earth. Because literary texts, in particular, speak to so much more than just our critical reason and typically deal with important, emotionally charged subjects, I, like many others, have students write journals each week. In them they can reflect on the emotions as well as the ideas generated by the material and class discussion. Then I respond each week, which takes considerable time but is important. The weekly back-and-forth written conversation acknowledges that the books and films we encounter are not merely "texts" to examine intellectually. They are also powerful multifaceted communications from other human beings — some long dead — that address real and often disturbing issues.

From student journals I have learned many things. Here is one: the abundance of progressive scholarship now available prepares liberal arts faculty to excel at teaching students how to identify and analyze many social injustices. We call attention to racism, misogyny, environmental devastation, economic inequity, religious intolerance, homophobia, colonialism, and more. Often, we are also excellent at showing how we are all implicated in these systems of oppression. And there we stop. We leave our students enlightened but so overwhelmed at the magnitude of what's wrong that they see no way of reacting except with despair or withdrawal. In my experience many students desperately want to translate progressive analyses into positive social action, but we fail to give them workable theory and tools.

As one student wrote in her first response paper in a course I taught a few years ago titled Multicultural America before 1860, she saw a definite link between our early-nineteenth-century texts by African Americans and the shameful treatment of Hurricane Katrina victims in New Orleans. She then reflected on a student meeting she attended. She wrote that she hoped

> to discuss the socioeconomic truths brought to light by the Hurricane (ie: how the majority left behind were black and *all* who were left behind were poor) and my opinions were validated and strengthened. Yet I left the meeting not feeling empowered by the vindication, but angry, sad, frustrated, hopeless, and helpless instead. We know these power struggles exist and that the poor are marginalized, but what we don't know is what do we *do* about it after we recognize the problem? What can I, a college girl of relative privilege in the northeast, do to help the large (and growing) number of poor people in this country, or any other minority, for that matter? It would be really nice if someone could explain how to change the barriers after identifying them.

Perhaps humanities faculty assume that students are learning elsewhere how to move from critique to activism, what works and what does not when progressive social change is the goal. But I think no one is doing that teaching. Certainly the liberal arts are not. Further, I think activist literary texts, a category that defines a huge amount of American literature, as I will turn to in the next chapter, texts written to name and expose injustice and motivate readers to work for social transformation, ask us to go beyond critique to the concrete issue of change and how to achieve it. It is the job of liberal humanists to address that challenge in our courses.

IN A VALUABLE ESSAY on people's complicity in the power relations that produce oppression, Joel Pfister argues for incorporating "agency studies" into the classroom. He says teachers need to remind students that they as human beings have agency and are not merely victims or coerced colluders. I agree but advocate more. I believe we need not only to remind students that they have agency but also to teach them how to use that agency as progressive activists.

Graduate school training plus the pedagogical culture of most academic departments in the United States explicitly tell humanists not to bridge the gap between intellectual analysis and social action. We may do so outside of class, privately and personally, but not in the classroom. I disagree with that detachment. Drawing on the work of social activists and various other thinkers plus my own teaching experience, I am saying that progressive humanists need to create explicit instructional units on activism. Curricular units will vary for different people. But as I will share at several points in the chapters that follow, for me activism pedagogy includes theory, attention to process, identification of models, brainstorming about options, and individual or collaborative projects, determined and executed by the students themselves, that try out some sort of concrete activism outside the classroom. Not to provide this instruction disserves students who wish to connect their learning to the world but almost always lack knowledge about how to do that. It also violates the progressive activist texts that so many cherish in the American literary tradition, texts that certainly demand more from readers than just analysis.

Cynicism really comes out of despair, but the antidote to cynicism is not optimism but action. And action is finally born out of hope. Try to remember that. — Jim Wallis, *God's Politics*

# TWO

## What David Walker and Harriet Beecher Stowe Still Have to Teach Us

*"Not agitate!"* African American author and editor Pauline Hopkins exclaims in her piece titled "Monroe Rogers" in the *Colored American Magazine* in 1902. "Republics exist only on the tenure of being constantly agitated" (276). With these words Hopkins ends her biography of a black man unjustly extradited to North Carolina from Massachusetts despite angry, well-organized protests by African American and white activists. Even in the face of a defeat as bitter as Rogers's remand to the overtly racist courts of the Jim Crow South, Hopkins refused to entertain hopelessness.

The activist tradition in American literature is one of passionate critique — the calling out of injustice, the naming of violation upon violation of the principles of human equality and respect for the creation that the nation claims to honor. It is also a tradition of profound hope and idealism, belief that the people can and will hear, think, and take action to bring positive change. The tradition maintains that people can choose to lead their lives differently, persuade others to do likewise, and demand that the body politic redress injustices and commit — *really commit* — to the nation's frequently announced self-definition as an enlightened, inclusive, democratic society.

Past and present American literature teems with the energy of dissent and anger *and* idealism and a call to action. It is filled with belief that people can resolve individually and collectively to work for progressive social change. William Apess, David Walker, Lydia Maria Child, Ralph Waldo Emerson, Henry David Thoreau, Harriet Beecher Stowe, Frederick Douglass, Harriet Jacobs, Harriet E. Wilson, Elizabeth Stuart Phelps, Mark Twain, Sarah Winnemucca, William Dean Howells, Edward Bellamy, Charlotte Perkins Gilman, Charles Chesnutt, Pauline Elizabeth Hopkins, W. E. B. Du Bois, Zitkala-Ša, Sui Sin Far, Upton Sinclair, María Cristina Mena, Anzia Yezierska, Sinclair Lewis, Jean Toomer, Langston Hughes, Richard Wright — and the list, merely sketched here, continues unbroken into our own time with Helena María Viramontes, Leslie Marmon Silko, Wendell Berry, Alice Walker, Karen Tei Yamashita, Simon Ortiz, Martín Espada, Adrienne Rich, and countless others. All of these writers — and scores more — know that words contribute to liberal change. To be sure, they write to express themselves, to give us pleasure in the beauty and power of language, and to tell compelling stories. But they also write to expose what's wrong in the world, to affirm what is right and good, and, in every case whether explicitly or implicitly, to ask us not simply to understand but to act.

The activist call may be overt, as in the case of Lydia Maria Child, Harriet Wilson, Zitkala-Ša, Wendell Berry, and dozens more. Or it may operate more subtly. Can we read Toni Morrison's *Beloved* and not ask what is still to be done to confront the terrible legacy of slavery in the United States? Can we read Louise Erdrich's many novels and not ask why this nation continues to turn a blind eye to anti-Indian racism? Some of the nation's great literature calls us to account blatantly — Handsome Lake's *How America Was Discovered*, Sinclair Lewis's *Babbitt*, James Baldwin's *The Fire Next Time*, Janice Mirikitani's *Shedding Silence*, Leslie Marmon Silko's *Almanac of the Dead*. Other works do so more indirectly — Mark Twain's *Pudd'nhead Wilson*, Nella Larsen's *Passing*, Marilynne Robinson's *Housekeeping*, Sherman Alexie's *Reservation Blues*. And these categories of overt and indirect blur, of course. The point is that a broad spectrum of progressive vantage points and voices exists, ranging from in-your-face critique and direct activist appeals to more oblique representation and implied hopes for change. Taken together, this activist tradition constitutes a progressive tradition of American literature to be read not simply for its beauty and wisdom but also for its inspiration in the ongoing activist struggle for social justice and planetary sanity.

## Metacomet

*My crime's being an Indian.*
*What's yours?*
— Leonard Peltier, *Prison Writings*

On the Fourth of July in 1833 the Commonwealth of Massachusetts jailed Pequot writer, activist, and Methodist preacher William Apess for disturbing the peace. Author of five books and many speeches by 1837, the point at which he disappears from print history, Apess was charged with the crime of fomenting and leading the Mashpee Revolt.

That revolt consisted of the Wampanoag people in Mashpee, Massachusetts, demanding several things. They wanted the same right of self-rule enjoyed by other towns in the commonwealth, they wanted whites to quit stealing wood and hay from their land, and they did not want Harvard College to impose a white minister on them. Although Apess did not actually lead the revolt, which succeeded, he did play a major role. It's not surprising that the commonwealth charged him with "riot, assault, and trespass," sentenced him to thirty days in jail, and levied the enormous fine of $100. The governors of Massachusetts feared the power of his words. Apess's speeches and tracts had already inspired the *Liberator*, Boston's famous activist newspaper edited by abolitionist William Lloyd Garrison, to champion the Mashpee struggle.

Apess's "An Indian's Looking-Glass for the White Man" confronts the United States in the early 1830s with a scathing look at its anti-Indian racism. It asks the reader to picture all people in one assembly. Then Apess asks which race would have the most national crimes written upon its skin. "Can you charge the Indians with robbing a nation almost of their whole continent, and murdering their women and children, and then depriving the remainder of their lawful rights, that nature and God require them to have? And to cap the climax, rob another nation to till their grounds and welter out their days under the lash with hunger and fatigue under the scorching rays of a burning sun?" (157). As Robert Warrior emphasizes in *The People and the Word*, Apess calls out American racism and makes obvious the genocide targeting of Native people. He reverses the mirror to expose the glaring crimes of white America. With two simple rhetorical questions Apess lists the multiple charges: murder, land theft, kidnapping, denial of civil rights, torture.

In agreement, Lydia Maria Child, a white woman kicked out of the Boston Athenaeum for her outspoken views, angrily stated at the time: "We certainly have done all we could to secure the deadly hostility of the red man and the black man everywhere" (32). Her words echo today in Jim Wallis's *The Soul of Politics*: "The United States of America was established as a white society, founded upon the near-genocide of one race and then the enslavement of yet another" (98). Wallis adds: "These founding events of the American nations are not just historical. They also have theological and spiritual meaning. The systematic violence, both physical and spiritual, committed first against indigenous people and then against black Africans was, indeed, the original sin of the American nations. In other words, the United States of America was conceived in iniquity" (100–01). A preacher himself, Apess indicted America on exactly the same grounds two centuries ago. In the assembly of nations pictured by him, white America stands in the dock accused of violating both human and divine law. Apess clearly states that the nation originated in a double paradigm of violence and criminality: genocide and theft directed against indigenous people, enslavement and torture of blacks. Too often thought of today only in terms of a white/black paradigm, the foundational race crime that marks the United States, Apess insists and others, past and present, echo, is white/red as well as white/black. The two occurred simultaneously, working in concert, and neither has been expiated nor is simply a truth of the past.

Anticipating the American Indian Movement of the later twentieth century as well as the ongoing fight for indigenous self-determination today, Apess's "Looking-Glass" rejects racist definitions of Native Americans as inferior. He expresses pride in being an Indian, reminds readers that Jesus was not white, and all but laughs at the blasphemy of white supremacist thinking: "If black or red skins or any other skin of color is disgraceful to God, it appears that he has disgraced himself a great deal — for he has made fifteen colored people to one white and placed them here upon this earth. . . . Or have you the folly to think that the white man, being one in fifteen or sixteen, are the only beloved images of God?" (157). He also calmly insists on the right of Native men to marry whomever they wish, including white women.

Given Christianity's long history of oppressing Native people, Apess's position as Christian and indigenous almost always surprises my students. Yet as Jace Weaver explains of our own era, "Christianity can be for some a Native religion" (34). There is no one way to be either Native or Christian. At the same time, as Robert Warrior argues, it has to be understood that the basic text of Christian liberation theology, the Exodus story, presents huge problems. A narrative about God delivering chosen people from captivity by relocating them on someone else's land is, as Warrior puts it in "Canaanites, Cowboys, and Indians," "an inappropriate way for Native Americans to think about liberation" (95). Of that story Warrior says, "As a member of the Osage Nation of American Indians who stands in solidarity with other tribal people around the world, I read the Exodus stories with Canaanite eyes" (95), which is to say, from the point of view of the people brutally displaced. How and whether indigeneity and Christianity can be compatible, as James Treat and Andrea Smith discuss, is subject to debate. Certainly it is impossible, from a twenty-first-century perspective, to know with any conviction what Christianity did or did not provide for Apess personally. What is clear is that he courageously used it to call the nation on its hypocrisy, declaring in "An Indian's Looking-Glass": "If you can find a spirit like Jesus Christ and his Apostles prevailing now in any of the white congregations, I should like to know it" (158). Joining abolition theology in his day and anticipating liberation theology in ours, he casts Christianity's tenets back on it to expose injustice and call for action.

My emphasis on Apess's use of Christianity — like my emphasis on Christianity throughout much of this chapter — reflects history. It does not signal any interest on my part in pushing for some sort of Christian orientation to the humanities. As my heavy reliance on Native American beliefs and secular ethics in chapters 4 and 5 makes obvious, I believe that progressive activism can and does come from many sources. Apess, writing and speaking in the 1830s, reasoned from the point of view of the dominant faith tradition of the United States at the time, which was Christianity, as it remains for many today. He drew on it fiercely and fearlessly in his demand for justice and change.

Most radical is Apess's last published piece, *Eulogy on King Philip, as Pronounced at the Odeon, in Federal Street, Boston* (1836), delivered on the 160th anniversary of the death of Metacomet, the Pequot leader known to whites as King Philip. Metacomet's body was dismembered and his head displayed for twenty years on a stake at Plymouth, Massachusetts, following whites' massacre of Native men, women, and children in their settlement on the Mystic River. Apess extols him as a hero and a martyr. He praises the insurgent acts of an Indian leader fighting back against the U.S. government at a time when that government was forcing indigenous people at gunpoint onto reservations west of the Mississippi River. Adding to that militancy, as Barry O'Connell points out, is Apess's repeated juxtaposition of Metacomet and George Washington. He makes the two equals, at the very least, and calls the Pequot leader "the greatest man that ever lived upon the American shores" (290). Which raises a fundamental question. Whom should we honor as the true patriot, the true father of a country founded in revolution against cruel imperial power? And behind that question is an even more profound one. What might the United States look like — how might the people act, live, pray, think, raise their children, treat one another, regard the earth, dwell in balance with their nonhuman relatives — if Metacomet rather than General Washington stood as America's founding father?

Apess's eulogy for Metacomet, dead for more than a century when Apess spoke in Boston, eulogizes the world that could have been. *And it prophesies.* It envisions a different history — one that reveres rather than reviles Metacomet — to remind us of our ability to refuse lies and create a different future, if we have the courage.

## Abolition

There can be no justice without memory—without remembering the horrible crimes committed against humanity and the great human struggles for justice. —James Cone, *Risks of Faith*

When David Walker wrote his *Appeal, in Four Articles* in 1829 and Harriet Beecher Stowe published *Uncle Tom's Cabin* in 1852, neither knew if, when, or whether slavery would end in the United States. They argued passionately — vehemently — against an institution that in one form or another had prevailed throughout all known human history and across cultures. Yet they believed their words and actions could produce change.

Looking back, we argue that the end of chattel slavery in the southern states of the United States was inevitable. From Walker's and Stowe's vantage points in the late 1820s and early 1850s, however, no such clarity existed. They did not know what we in hindsight can calmly analyze as destiny. Indeed, if either or both had died at birth, who is to say that slavery would have been abolished in the United States? Such a question may sound crazy. So many complex factors of economics, politics, psychology, and history came into play to bring an end to slavery in the United States that the facts make clear that no one or two voices could possibly matter. But as Awiakta says in *Selu*, a book dedicated to trying to reeducate Western thinkers before we destroy human life on the planet, we need to expand our concepts of fact and truth. Words do have the ability to transform people and affect events. What David Walker and Harriet Beecher Stowe still have to teach us is that they were right: activist anger *and hope* do change the world.

ALTHOUGH MY STUDENTS have heard of (but rarely read) *Uncle Tom's Cabin*, they almost always know nothing about David Walker. So when I assigned his *Appeal* in a small seminar titled Boston Radicals, I looked forward to their responses. To my surprise, I encountered silence. Finally, one brave young white man admitted: "He's so angry. It's so out of control. I think it would be more effective if it weren't so full of anger — and so long." A white woman added: "He stereotypes all whites as horrible people. He's too extreme." Others from various racial locations nodded in agreement. Their reactions made me think of Harvard professor William James in 1903 asking his former student W. E. B. Du Bois why *The Souls of Black Folk* was so negative.

Part of the problem comes from students' ignorance about slavery. They know it existed, was wrong, got abolished, and left a bitter legacy. But what it actually consisted of, its presence in the Americas for centuries as a state-sanctioned system of race-based human torture at every level, that knowledge in any vivid, immediate way they lack. Because of good educational programs in many U.S. schools the young people I teach know more about the decades of the Nazi holocaust than the centuries of legal mutilation, rape, murder, kidnap, and degradation of people of African descent in the Americas. Slavery has become comfortable knowledge in the United States, something people unite in condemning but, finally, have few details about. For my students, the rage of David Walker did not attach to specifics, which meant I needed to provide a great deal more historical context.

However, another part of the problem comes not from ignorance but from overload. Teachers frequently lament students' ignorance (for which we ought to be grateful, of course, since our jobs depend on it), but also, throwing up their hands in disgust, progressives often criticize students' resistance to difficult truths, their desire to avoid looking at and thinking about the terrible things in the world that people have done and do. But the students are right. The world they are inheriting from us is terrifying. The seas are rising, genocide proceeds unchecked in poor parts of the globe, multinational corporations are genetically altering seeds, entire ecosystems are being eradicated, children are bought and sold around the world for sex, pandemics hover. Many of my students are in denial — they try to avoid taking in yet more horrible information — out of self-preservation. They already know of countless unthinkable things in the world over which they believe they have no control. Why should they welcome news of more? Their resistance I now recognize as a sign of mental health, at least in many cases, and believe it comes in part from our failure in the humanities to offer hope and concrete ways to translate critical analysis into progressive activist change. If humanities study consists of nothing but showing how horrendous the world has been and is and the limitations of human beings' efforts to change it (and, of course, we *are* limited), how much can we expect the young to absorb? And why? For what purpose?

We need to tell our students, because it is the truth, that the world could not have looked darker to David Walker or Harriet Beecher Stowe than it does to us today. Then we need literally to say to them, as I do, If William Apess or David Walker or Harriet Beecher Stowe did not give in to feelings of powerlessness and despair, can we? Can we in good conscience enjoy the privilege of being able to read and write and know where our next meal will come from and not use our words to advocate for social and planetary justice? The work of the humanities is intellectual, true. But it is also moral and spiritual. *And practical.* The fact is that liberal humanists *do* believe that ideas and words actually affect human life and the life of the planet. If we did not believe that, few of us would devote our energy to the odd lifelong work of reading, teaching, and writing about ideas and words. Yet too many progressive teachers shy away from talking head-on about the power of the humanities, and literature in particular, to contribute to the activist struggle for progressive social change by transforming people's minds and hearts. There are reasons for the reticence — embarrassment about displaying emotion, fear of neoconservative censors (who are out there), brainwashing by contemporary postmodernist theory, discouragement born of setbacks. However, as much feminist, antiracist, economic justice, gay and lesbian, indigenous, and ecocritical pedagogy over the last three decades has continued to insist, it is important to emphasize the transformative power of words and ideas if we wish to prepare young people for the work of the world.

The full title of David Walker's appeal in its third and final edition is *Appeal, in Four Articles; Together with A Preamble, To the Coloured Citizens of the World, but In Particular, and Very Expressly, To Those of the United States of America.* This detailed wording forecasts a calm, measured document of persuasion neatly organized into four parts, complete with preamble — nothing unusual. The opening, *"My dearly beloved Brethren and Fellow Citizens,"* likewise signals the discussion will be gentle, even sweet. Nothing prepares us for the fury, the rage, that makes every page explosive and declares that the only possible way for a black man to speak of the horror of slavery — a horror beyond imagining at every level, physical, spiritual, and moral — is to write with flame. No calm, measured way to speak exists.

Walker's not-measured way of speaking is also brilliantly strategic. Rhetorically, the *Appeal* defines itself as a revolutionary document, a militant call for rebellion that blatantly parallels the seminal sacred text of the nation, the Declaration of Independence. Lest we miss that fact, Walker virtually shouts at the end:

> See your Declaration Americans! ! ! Do you understand your own language? Hear your language, proclaimed to the world, July 4th, 1776 — ☛ "We hold these truths to be self evident — that ALL MEN ARE CREATED EQUAL! ! that they *are endowed by their Creator with certain unalienable rights*; that among these are life, *liberty*, and the pursuit of happiness! !" Compare your own language above, extracted from your Declaration of Independence, with your cruelties and murders inflicted by your cruel and unmerciful fathers and yourselves on our fathers and on us — men who have never given your fathers or you the least provocation! ! ! ! !

Walker's black Declaration of Independence quotes further from the national treasure: "But when a long train of abuses and usurpation, pursuing invariably the same object, evinces a design to reduce them under absolute despotism, it is their *right*, it is their *duty*, to throw off such government" (75). Like Apess in fearlessly attacking white racism, Walker writes to incite revolt. He writes to change the world, to foment violent retaliation for three hundred years of systematic, legal, Christian genocide, torture, and state-sanctioned terrorism against enslaved people of African descent in North America.

What is too long—too many words, too many pages—for that subject? I asked my students. Why do we revere a white declaration of violent revolution and shrink from a black one? What is too unnuanced in the representation of white people when it comes to slavery in the United States, a race-based institution that oppressed millions to benefit whites? Walker does not stereotype white people. He identifies what white means in the paradigm of U.S. slavery. It means oppressor, torturer, profiteer, murderer, rapist, and religious hypocrite, as Harriet Beecher Stowe, Henry David Thoreau, Frederick Douglass, Martin Delaney, Lydia Maria Child, Angelina Grimke, Harriet Jacobs, William Lloyd Garrison, Frances Ellen Harper, Wendell Phillips, and thousands of other abolitionists agreed and picked up their pens to assert as well. As we talked the group discarded the concept of "too angry" when speaking of an institution that defines the speaker as not human and labels the act of castrating him, cutting his tongue out, whipping him to death, and raping his mother as *legal*. Words, they started to realize, must be inflamed to convey such a reality.

IN ADDITION TO its justice language, Walker's *Appeal* uses a holy rhetoric. As Jim Wallis cautions in *The Soul of Politics*, "It is a popular mistake to think all evangelicals are cast in the Pat Robertson mold. Most African Americans are evangelical Christians, as were many abolitionists" (x), a point that Cornel West likewise emphasizes in *Democracy Matters*: "The most influential social movements for justice in America have been led by prophetic Christians: the abolitionist, women's suffrage, and trade-union movements in the nineteenth century and the civil rights movement in the twentieth century" (152). West oversimplifies. Some in these movements were not Christians or were so in no deep, committed way. Still, his point, like Wallis's, bears reflecting on. In West's view the prophetic strains of Christianity, by which he means the progressive tradition committed to social justice, "represent the democratic ideal of religion in public life" (152). Especially in the current era of right-wing Christian fundamentalism, he believes that liberal prophetic voice is needed more than ever.

Walker's liberal prophetic voice in the *Appeal*, written almost two hundred years ago by a man denied the vote and who could be captured and sold at any moment, animates a black jeremiad. Named for the Old Testament prophet Jeremiah, the jeremiad has been an honored sermon form from the Puritan pulpit to Malcolm X to many evangelicals today. It consists of angry excoriation of injustice and a visionary call to judgment. Walker's draws down God's fury on white America for the sin of slavery. All prophets deal in dangerous speech. They brave the wrath of powerful worldly leaders; they expose revered figures as liars, hypocrites, and sinners, in Walker's case attacking Thomas Jefferson and Henry Clay specifically; and they foretell God's fearful verdict on those who break the divine commandments. As the contemporary black liberation theologian James Cone points out in *Risks of Faith*, black Christianity in the United States, far from functioning as an opiate, has played an indispensable part in the African American activist struggle for freedom. Certainly David Walker, drawing on that tradition, knew that his words could cost him his life, and he was right. Southern planters put a price on his head. Many believe his mysterious death from poisoning outside his Boston home soon after the third and last publication of the *Appeal* in 1830 resulted from a murder plot.

Prophetic speech names sin, assigns blame, and predicts divine judgment. It is not "maybe" or "perhaps" or feel-good speech. It is harsh, absolute, and emphatic. It *knows*. In the righteous it enables courage and action. In the guilty it inspires fear and defensiveness. Most people do not want to hear prophets. They want to argue with them, quibble, find excuses, reveal flaws in their logic and command of facts. Prophets do not care. Walker did not care. Prophets know they are right; Walker knew he was right. As Cornel West observes in *Democracy Matters*, which refers to Walker's *Appeal* along with liberatory texts by Lydia Maria Child, Herman Melville, Ralph Waldo Emerson, Walt Whitman, W. E. B. Du Bois, James Baldwin, and Toni Morrison, one of the most important weapons in the fight against early-twenty-first-century antidemocratic dogmas of free-market fundamentalism, aggressive militarism, and mounting authoritarianism is precisely this Judaic tradition of prophetic witness. Along with Socratic questioning and what he calls tragicomic hope, this prophetic tradition, West argues, plays a major role in forcing elites to change. In reply to pessimists he states simply: "But our history has shown they can be forced" (33).

Drafting a black Declaration of Independence and speaking in the long-honored tradition of the jeremiad, David Walker castigates fellow blacks who collude and cower — "Oh! my coloured brethren, all over the world, when shall we arise from this death-like apathy? — And be men!!" (62) — and damns the whites who hold slaves or do nothing to end the institution — "Does not the blood of our fathers and of us their children, cry aloud to the Lord of Sabaoth against you, for the cruelties and murders with which you have, and do continue to afflict us" (5–6). His jeremiad is one of the great patriotic texts of the nation.

SO TOO Harriet Beecher Stowe more than two decades later wrote to inspire radical change. First published in installments in 1851–52 in a small antislavery newspaper, *Uncle Tom's Cabin* in book form in 1852 instantly became a phenomenon. It kept printing presses running day and night, outsold every book except the Bible throughout the nineteenth century, circled the globe in numerous editions and translations, generated a virtual industry of sensationalized traveling Tom shows and consumer products, and permanently entered the national mythology as one of the United States' great — and most controversial — books. As Thomas Gossett and many others note, the novel has never produced indifference. Southern slaveholders charged that it was full of lies; abolitionists praised it but debated specifics; President Lincoln, so the story goes, greeted its author at the White House as "the little woman who started the Great War"; generations of writers, black and white, imitated its strategies; Langston Hughes wrote a complimentary introduction to a twentieth-century reissue and James Baldwin attacked it as racist; and many white women scholars have in recent years argued that it contains a valuable narrative of alternative feminist values.

As activism, *Uncle Tom's Cabin* is an evangelical political conversion text. Written by a woman whose father, brother, husband, and sons were preachers and who clearly would have entered the ministry herself had gender not barred her from the pulpit, the book does not simply use or invoke liberal Christianity. It recasts Jesus doubly — as a black man and as a white little girl — to exhort white readers to a fundamental change of heart and will. At an extremely bleak hour in the antislavery struggle, the years immediately following passage of the 1850 Fugitive Slave Act, which required every American, Northerner or Southerner, to turn in escaped slaves, *Uncle Tom's Cabin* passionately urges readers not to give up hope, not to despair. *Uncle Tom's Cabin* reflects back at white America, like Apess and Walker before Stowe, the enormity of the nation's perfidy. Also like their work, the novel testifies to its author's belief that words can and will make a crucial and concrete difference by inspiring and strengthening people in the activist struggle for justice.

In *The Battle for God* Karen Armstrong talks about two traditions of truth in the Western world, myth and logos. The first, she explains, is religious and the second, from the Enlightenment forward, secular. Academicians usually deal with logos, as we should. It is the business of education to concern itself with rational analysis and argument. But literary texts are not entirely rational. As Lawrence Buell points out in *Writing for an Endangered World,* narrative has the ability to generate feelings and show ethics in action, both of which have an impact on us. In addition to its intellectual force, in other words, literature operates on emotional and, frequently, spiritual levels as well. Those irrational dimensions people can and often do analyze rationally. Critics use psychoanalytic theory, for instance, to show how hidden narratives express unacknowledged desires and fears. But it is also important for liberal secular humanists to meet on their own ground the serious spiritual dynamics of activist texts such as Walker's and Stowe's.

Walker's *Appeal* and Stowe's *Uncle Tom's Cabin,* like much progressive activist writing in the United States, especially in the past, as Joycelyn Moody explains of many black women writers, do not use religion as a device. They constitute themselves foundationally as spiritual texts. They exist, to use Armstrong's distinction, as myth far more than as logos. They seek, like an evangelical sermon, to produce a conversion experience, to enact a spiritual revolution in the reader or listener that will result in a radical change in behavior: a new or a renewed commitment to work actively for social justice. In the parlance of contemporary evangelicalism, texts such as Walker's and Stowe's seek to produce in their reader or listener a born-again experience, a transformation.

Read only politically, or only intellectually, or only for their emotional impact (the intensity of anger in Walker's case, of grief in Stowe's), or only aesthetically, or only for their buried psychological scripts, all of which are approved academic ways of reading and each of which is interesting and valuable, these books get divorced from much of their activist power, which is finally spiritual.

This does not mean liberal humanists should advocate specific religious views or promote religion itself. Except for institutions that operate under the aegis of a particular religious organization, education must protect its secular independence, without which intellectual freedom cannot exist. Rather, I am saying that humanists need to take seriously the spiritual dimensions of activist literary texts such as *Uncle Tom's Cabin* and Walker's *Appeal* in order to comprehend the faith act that inspires and impels the activism of each, just as a different but no less profound faith act inspires and impels the activism of Karl Marx and Frederick Engels's *Communist Manifesto* and yet another informs Leonard Peltier's *Prison Writings*, subtitled *My Life Is My Sun Dance*. The spiritual basis of each of these must be admitted. Progressive political change often depends on activism made possible by strong belief in shared values and faith-based truths outside of and larger than oneself. For liberal humanists to ignore or sneer at religious truths, as some — though, of course, not all — do, is to assign ourselves an irrelevant or, worse, destructive role in the struggle for social and planetary justice.

AT ITS ACTIVIST CENTER *Uncle Tom's Cabin* rewrites the New Testament story of the crucifixion. If, as Armstrong argues, contemporary religious fundamentalism makes the mistake of reading literally what must be understood mythically or symbolically, Stowe makes no such error. Like Apess and Walker, she knows that Jesus was not a white man, and in *Uncle Tom's Cabin* he is not even singular or, in one of his two manifestations, male.

Stowe's black Christ is unmistakable. Tom is physically very strong, the father of many children, and incredibly courageous in the face of physical and psychic pain. Yet he is also, as I noted many years ago, distinctly feminized. He is gentle, loving, long-suffering, nonviolent, family oriented, deeply religious, and emotionally receptive and intuitive rather than hyperrational and intellectual. This feminization ties Tom to a network of mothers in *Uncle Tom's Cabin*, black and white, who resist slavery to the best of their ability. It associates him with the positive values of nineteenth-century domestic feminism and sentiment, which, as Jane Tompkins has persuasively argued, Stowe embraces and advocates in opposition to slavery.

But Tom's maternalization also marks him as a Christ figure. Beaten to death by Simon Legree, whose bullet head, iron fists, and hell-on-earth plantation clearly make him the satanic, grotesquely hypermasculine opposite of Tom, Stowe's black Christ, as loving and gentle and selfless as the perfect mother, consciously sacrifices his life to save others. Tom dies because he refuses to flog other slaves and will not give information about fugitives' escape route. Stowe titles chapter 40 (the number of weeks in most pregnancies and the number of days Jesus spent in the wilderness) "The Martyr" and parallels Tom's torture and death to Jesus's. Echoing Christ's words on the cross, "My God, my God, why hast thou forsaken me?" and "I thirst," Tom cries out, "O Jesus! Lord Jesus! have you quite forgot us poor critturs?" and "Help, Lord, I perish!" (329). Threatened with death for refusing to betray fellow slaves, he chooses to give his life: "Well, then, I *will* die!" (330). He looks heavenward and repeats word for word Christ's final words on the cross: "Into thy hands I commend my spirit!" (375).

Also and paradoxically (but Christianity is based on paradox), the feminization of Tom links him to Eva, Stowe's other and equally unexpected maternal Christ. The shortened form of her name — Eva — obviously evokes and redeems the biblical first mother even as the longer form — Evangeline — calls up Jesus, the supreme evangel; and the little white girl herself draws a clear parallel between Jesus's and her death when she says of the slaves on her deathbed, "I *would* die for them, Tom, if I could" (252). A martyr to the terrible national sin, this white girl/child Christ wastes away because of the horror of slavery. Her innocent death and the hope Stowe embeds in her dying wish to give her life for others predict the crucifixion of Tom, which climaxes the book, and his sacrifice serves as the supreme model of faith-based love and placing others first on which Stowe rests her argument for activist opposition to slavery.

IN *A KEY TO UNCLE TOM'S CABIN*, the compilation of sources and further argument that she published a year after *Uncle Tom's Cabin* to defend the verisimilitude of her novel and to advocate for abolition outright, Stowe titles a chapter "What Is to Be Done?" That is the urgent question of all of *Uncle Tom's Cabin*. What actions can be taken? What will lead to victory? What will bring an end to slavery?

Cornel West comments in *Prophetic Reflections* on the relationship between social analysis and activism for leftist Christians in the twentieth-century struggle to end apartheid in South Africa:

> As Christians, we wish to employ social analysis from the vantage point of society's victims, from the vantage point of those who suffer, from the vantage point of the Cross, the Christocentric perspective. Therefore the types of social analyses we would deploy

not only attempt to interpret the world but also attempt to isolate potentialities for ultimate realization in struggle.

Accordingly, we must note that our overall discursive context is a battle. Here is one of the few places I agree with John Calvin: human history is in fact a battleground for struggle, contestation, conflict, and resistance. The question is not only on what side are you but also how you understand the side that you are on such that you can ultimately triumph. The aim is to win, to expand the scope of democracy, to expand the scope of individuals who have a status of sanctity and dignity. In this sense, social analysis is a weapon, a tool, an instrument for struggle. This is very important because a lot of our secular comrades, especially on the left, tend to make social analysis and tools of social analysis themselves fetishes and idols. Whereas, for Christians, social analyses serve simply as tools and instruments. (186)

Like West in knowing she occupies a battleground and that social analysis is only a tool, not an end in itself, Stowe presents Christ crucified in the United States in the twinned innocents, Eva and Tom. This is not some interesting abstract intellectual exercise. It is the basis for a call to action. All of *Uncle Tom's Cabin* forces readers and listeners to the question of the *Key* — "What Is to Be Done?" — which is also the question Stowe poses at the end of the novel and the question, like many in our own time, that seemed so huge and daunting that many viewed it as unanswerable.

Perhaps for that reason the closing pages of *Uncle Tom's Cabin* address the reader directly. Stowe states point-blank that descriptions of slavery cannot come close to the full horror of the reality. She then turns immediately to the issue of action: "And now, men and women of

America, is this a thing to be trifled with, apologized for, and passed over in silence?" (403). What can people do? First and above all, Stowe says, refuse to remain silent. Especially she beseeches free white mothers — Americans like herself who in 1852 lacked basic civil rights, the ballot, or even reproductive control over their own bodies — *not to remain silent.* The disempowered, Stowe believes no less than Apess, Walker, West, Cone, Cannon, and Wallis, can speak. She implores: "By the sick hour of your child; by those dying eyes, which you can never forget; by those last cries, that wrung your heart when you could neither help nor save; by the desolation of that empty cradle, that silent nursery, — I beseech you, pity those mothers that are constantly made childless by the American slave-trade! And say, mothers of America, is this a thing to be defended, sympathized with, passed over in silence?" (404). Between the novel and the *Key* Stowe offers many concrete suggestions for action: pray, make reparations to free blacks, fight racism in the North in one's community, gain accurate knowledge about slavery, give money to the black church, teach white children the truth, support ministers in the North who preach abolition, and personally mount uncompromising arguments against slavery at every possible opportunity, including in the South. Two things run fiercely through all of this advice: belief in spiritual faith as the foundation for liberatory activism and belief in the power of words.

Stowe asks at the end of *Uncle Tom's Cabin*, "But, what can any individual do?" She answers, "Of that, every individual can judge" and then immediately adds: "There is one thing that every individual can do, — they can see to it that *they feel right.* An atmosphere of sympathetic influence encircles every human being; and the man or woman who *feels* strongly, healthily and justly, on the great interests of humanity, is a constant benefactor to the human race. See, then," she admonishes, "to your sympathies in this matter! Are they in harmony with the sympathies of Christ? or are they swayed and perverted by the sophistries of worldly policy?" (404–05). Far from the naive statement it might first appear (we are going to *feel* our way out of injustice?), Stowe's call-to-action recognizes the bottom-line enemies of progressive change: numbness, indifference, denial, selfishness, cynicism. Activism in the service of social justice requires more than intellect. It requires righteous anger, empathy, faith, and hope.

Those last two — faith and hope — Stowe knows can ring hollow in the ears of the oppressed. She repeatedly has George Harris, Tom's militant counterpart in *Uncle Tom's Cabin*, inveigh against the idea that the United States will ever change or that Christianity, the apologizer for slavery, can possibly lead the nation in the fight for freedom. His arguments are so powerful and well understood by Stowe and his rage so warranted that, though he lives and Tom dies, she can't imagine what to do with him as a free man in America. She ships him along with all other resistant free blacks to Liberia at the end of the novel. Stowe wants revolution to be peaceful. She fears it cannot be, as her 1856 antislavery novel about black-led revolution, *Dred, a Tale of the Great Dismal Swamp*, imagines and then backs away from. Even in *Uncle Tom's Cabin* she admits and justifies the role of violence — she compares George Harris to a Hungarian freedom fighter and shows a Quaker abolitionist approving the taking up of arms to defend Eliza Harris and her baby as they escape through Ohio. But in the tradition of William Lloyd Garrison in her day and Mahatma Gandhi and Martin Luther King, Jr., a century later, Stowe hopes for peaceful social transformation.

UNCLE TOM'S CABIN is not a perfect book, any more than Walker's is. He castigates people enslaved for generations for not having the resources or will to resist masters whose power was virtually omnipotent, and she did not always live up to her own advice. Susan Belasco, like others, rightly notes Stowe's failure to respond positively to requests for assistance, for instance, from both Frederick Douglass and Harriet Jacobs. And the novel itself, as many have argued, including me, reinforces racial stereotypes. Further, its endorsement of African colonization, Stowe's dispatch to Liberia of all of the narrative's defiant free blacks, including and especially George Harris, upset abolitionists at the time and continues to damage the text's vision of U.S. democracy. But the parable of resistance at the center of the novel, the belief that even the most horrific systems of human injustice can be met with moral refusal and an alternative activist ethic grounded in spiritual values based in love and predicated on hope, remains of tremendous value to progressive struggle.

Stowe, writing in 1852, could not see the route to victory. What it took to end slavery was a civil war, the type of violence she was trying not to endorse. In another way, however, she was prescient. Although the Civil War and the Emancipation Proclamation officially abolished slavery, the system she wrote against has not really ended. Contemporary liberal spiritual thinkers such as James Cone, Jim Wallis, Cornel West, Katie Cannon, and Michael Lerner all argue that a fundamental revolution of mind and spirit when it comes to both race and economic inequity is still desperately needed in the United States. Cone maintains in *Risks of Faith* that all theology in the modern West must begin with the sin of racism. And reparations have never occurred. The activist spiritual transformation called for by *Uncle Tom's Cabin* has yet to happen.

# The Meaning of John Brown

The first step along the path [Chief Wilma Mankiller] indicates is to examine what needs to be done and to think about it, think not only with the intellect but also with a fusion of heart, mind and soul — to think purposefully.
—Awiakta, *Selu*

James Cone reminds us in *Risks of Faith* that Martin Luther King, Jr., was a public theologian. People tend to choose either Dr. King the preacher or Dr. King the civil rights activist, but Cone explains that the two must not be separated. King could not have been true to his faith if he had not been an activist for social justice. He could not have acted if he did not have his faith.

So, too, people tend to choose their Thoreau. They make him the nature writer, the solitary lover of the environment who lived for a while in a hut at Walden Pond, or the advocate of passive resistance, the activist who spent a night in jail rather than pay his poll tax to a government that countenanced slavery. He becomes either the author of *Walden* (1854) or the author of "Resistance to Civil Government" (1849), popularly known as *Civil Disobedience*. But, in fact, as with Martin Luther King, Henry David Thoreau was not divided against himself. His two best-known works spring from the same moral center, the same belief system, which was at its core profoundly spiritual though emphatically not Christian or conformist to any other orthodoxy.

Thoreau wrote *Walden* because he was an activist dissenter, and he was an activist dissenter because he was strengthened and guided by his powerful belief in the sacredness of all planetary life. The same refusal to accept what we call conventional wisdom, ideas in his time about the impossibility of ever ending slavery or of the earth as an inexhaustible resource existing for the sole purpose of being exploited by human beings, inspires the nature writing and the political activist pieces. When Thoreau says in *Walden*, "The government of the world I live in was not framed, like that of Britain, in after-dinner conversations over wine" (263), he is speaking of his life in the woods, his personal, moral, and spiritual choice not to live as society expects (work, marry, procreate, accumulate material possessions). But the statement applies as easily to his political resistance. For when he asks in *Civil Disobedience*, speaking of his refusal to obey the U.S. government because it condones slavery, "Must the citizen ever for a moment, or in the least degree, resign his conscience to the legislator? Why has every man a conscience, then?" (18), he is stating the same truth. Thoreau tried to live and write what Chief Mankiller means when she says activism must begin in purposeful thought, thought that is not merely intellectual but instead fuses heart, mind, and soul. This kind of thought Awiakta identifies as walking in one's soul. Immersion in such thought at Walden Pond and speaking out for justice went hand in hand for Thoreau. No contradiction existed between his meticulously revising his final edition of *Walden*, as the activist scholar Paul Lauter points out, at the same time that he was preparing and delivering his furious Fourth of July speech for the 1854 Antislavery Convention in Framingham, Massachusetts, "Slavery in Massachusetts."

That speech is a secular jeremiad. Invited to address the righteous (who but the converted would be at an antislavery convention?), Thoreau upbraids the audience for its hypocrisy, the audacity of Massachusetts abolitionists condemning Southern slaveholders while their own commonwealth places on trial an escaped slave to decide if he is a human being or property to be shipped south. Echoing Frederick Douglass's famous 1852 "What to the Slave Is the Fourth of July?" Thoreau jeers at Independence Day celebrations in his birthplace of Concord,

Massachusetts. He asks with anger and incredulity how citizens can ring bells and hang banners for liberty when millions are held in captivity in their own country. "Nowadays, men wear a fool's cap, and call it a liberty-cap" (393), he states in words that could come from *Walden*; and, referring to the Fugitive Slave Act, he attacks the mental and moral servility of citizens who bow to the idea that justice must wait on Supreme Court rulings. Judges and lawyers are not the arbiters. "They consider, not whether the Fugitive Slave Law is right, but whether it is what they call *constitutional*. Is virtue constitutional, or vice? Is equity constitutional, or inequity?" Thoreau exclaims. "I would remind my countrymen that they are to be men first, and Americans only at a late and convenient hour" (401). A higher law than patriotism exists. It is called truth, and it comes from what he identifies, deliberately *not* invoking God, as moral principles of justice and equity that surpass mere human law but can be known by anyone who has the courage to look inward.

Thoreau went to the woods, as is often quoted, to live deliberately, to separate himself from human society so that he might learn from the natural world and from the spiritual reservoirs within. In "Slavery in Massachusetts" he calls for group separation from civil society. Until Massachusetts dissolves its union with the slaveholding South by defying the Fugitive Slave Act, he believes it the duty of all abolitionists to dissolve their union with Massachusetts. Such resistance constitutes a moral imperative for Thoreau, who declares he has lost his country and entered hell. This happened, he tells the activists gathered on the Fourth of July, when "Massachusetts last deliberately sent back an innocent man, Anthony Burns, to slavery. I dwelt before, perhaps, in the illusion that my life passed somewhere only *between* heaven and hell, but now I cannot persuade myself that I do not dwell *wholly within* hell" (405). He marvels at fellow whites going about their business as if nothing is wrong and pronounces as he draws toward his conclusion that inaction threatens the liberty of all. Both the lives of enslaved Africans and the life of the nation hang in the balance.

Thoreau ends "Slavery in Massachusetts" with the hope not of God but of the natural world. The earth has taught him that there is power larger than our own in the creation. He watches a water lily: "It reminds me that Nature has been partner to no Missouri Compromise" (407–08). Linking nature and social justice, Thoreau says that the evil humans generate will finally be no more than manure to feed the water lily, which is simultaneously a flower and a reminder of "the purity and courage which are immortal" (408). Vine Deloria, Jr., Winona LaDuke, Marilou Awiakta, and so many others point out that indigenous people have always known and continue to know that the earth is sacred. Likewise, Thoreau believes we can learn from the earth how to live as part of the creation. Or we can choose to die.

THREE YEARS BEFORE his own death and with abolition still totally uncertain, Thoreau delivered his most vehement human rights address in 1859, "A Plea for John Brown." It reveres the imprisoned abolitionist pilloried as a madman and condemned as too violent by much of the nation. Rightly remembered around the world for *Civil Disobedience*, which inspired two of the twentieth century's great heroes in the struggle for human rights, Gandhi and Martin Luther King, Jr., Thoreau, we must also remember, did not endorse pacifism at any cost. He praises John Brown as a model of *militant* disobedience. He holds Brown up as an activist who embodies in armed fury *Walden*'s and *Civil Disobedience*'s shared denunciation of blind acquiescence in public opinion and obedience to convention and authority when those contradict morality.

Linck Johnson writes of "Thoreau's profound faith in words, in the power of a text to transform the lives of readers and, consequently, to reform the institutions of society" (53), and he is right. Ardent faith motivates all of Thoreau's work. Although he refused to subscribe to any specific religious doctrine or creed, he, along with other transcendentalists such as Emerson and Margaret Fuller, insisted that spirit permeates the universe, including human beings. He spoke and wrote in the belief that words can, as Johnson says, have a transformative effect that motivates people as activists in the service of social justice.

For Thoreau, John Brown epitomized justified violence against a system so horrible that Thoreau describes the entire United States in "A Plea for John Brown" as a slave ship "smothering four millions under the hatches" (424). Yet, he observes with disbelief, politicians preach patience and forbearance. Not John Brown. And not Thoreau, for whom the courageous Brown stands as a model: "He was a superior man. He did not value his bodily life in comparison with ideal things. He did not recognize unjust human laws, but resisted them as he was bid" (424). Clearly invoking *Walden*'s repeated question about whether, when death comes, one will actually have lived, Thoreau states of Brown as he faces execution: "It seems as if no man had ever died in America before; for in order to die you must first have lived" (434). Like Apess, Walker, and Stowe before him, Thoreau caustically attacks Christians. They praise Jesus yet condemn a man willing to give his life to free others. In the tradition of Apess's eulogizing Metacomet, Thoreau calls the man who fought slaveholding in bloody Kansas and attempted to lead a slave uprising at Harpers Ferry a greater patriot than Franklin or Washington.

MY STUDENTS DO NOT know who John Brown was — much less Metacomet. Most have heard the name John Brown; some can half-sing the jingle about him moldering in the grave; and sometimes someone vaguely recalls something about his being insane and violent. Beyond that they draw a blank. Since my job is to teach, I don't object to their need for knowledge. But it does make me reflect on what knowledge is being transmitted and what erased as well as what is at stake. When I ask students to list activists in the progressive struggle for justice in the United States, past and present, excluding elected officials and writers (they have a ready pool of those on my syllabus), they invariably generate a very short list. First always is Martin Luther King, Jr., then Rosa Parks, and then usually, in some order, Harriet Tubman, Frederick Douglass, Sojourner Truth, Malcolm X, and Susan B. Anthony, plus a scattering of others. I try out a few possibilities such as Crazy Horse, Victoria Woodhull, William Lloyd Garrison, Takao Ozawa, Emma Goldman, Russell Means, or César Chávez. Usually I meet little success beyond, sometimes, vague recognition of one or two. Asked to name at least five social justice activists from their own racial and gender location, past or present, almost no one can. On my campus a coveted prize is named for Wendell Phillips and given to the senior chosen to deliver the graduation address. Almost always, none of my students knows that Wendell Phillips was a radical white abolitionist whose speeches were so powerful that he attracted audiences in the thousands and had to carry a pistol for protection against proslavers' death threats.

U.S. history and American literature testify to an unbroken tradition of progressive, courageous activism by insurgents, dissidents, and radicals. Yet young people today, at least in my experience, too often regard each of those labels as negative. Several decades of right-wing propaganda have successfully taught people to apply those terms to enemies of freedom and democracy, as defined, of course, by that same right-wing propaganda, rather than to embrace them as foundational in the liberal struggle for justice in the United States from its founding to the present. When only a handful of social justice activists can be named, if that, with passive resistance the most (and often sole) esteemed strategy and African Americans vastly predominant, important as both are and have been, a clear lesson is being sent that contains and marginalizes progressive struggle. Blacks in the United States have in high percentages led the fight for equity and freedom, and that fact should never be ignored. But poor white farmers, Asian Americans, Latinos, birth control advocates, Native Americans of every nation, migrant workers, women of every race, union laborers, privileged white men of conscience, antiwar agitators, Catholics, Jews, Muslims, atheists, and countless others have also always filled the ranks of progressive dissent and vision in the United States. In addition, victory has not always come from passive resistance. Those facts also need to be emphasized.

To illustrate, in my course on multicultural U.S. literature before 1860 I include among many things Mexican American *corridos* from the 1850s, anonymous ballads now available in anthologies and created, as Raymond Paredes explains, "to celebrate those border Mexicans from either side of the Río Grande who resisted Anglo injustice" (35). I also include letters to the editor written by Chinese merchants in San Francisco in the same decade. Some of the letters were published in an 1852 pamphlet titled *An Analysis of the Chinese Question*, which contains a letter of support signed by a group of white merchants, and others appeared in 1855 in the bilingual newspaper the *Oriental*. All are available only in photocopy because they have never been reprinted, and all firmly refute the anti-Asian racism of California governor John Bigler.

The merchants rebut Bigler's argument that immigration from Asia must be stopped. They reject his criticisms that Chinese immigrants take jobs from whites, band together in their own communities, send their money back to China, and differ essentially from Europeans. Hab Wa and Long Achick, signing for the group of merchants in 1852, point out that Chinese immigrants work side by side with whites and live together to provide support for each other. They send money back to their families in China just as immigrants from Europe always have, and they do not differ essentially from white Americans, a point the merchants underscore, unfortunately, by racistly denigrating Native Americans. The authors punctuate their case with barbed remarks that mock the governor: "We do not deny that many Chinamen tell lies, and so do many Americans, even in Courts of Justice" (8). As my students read these letters, they see for themselves a number of things. Racism in the United States has never operated simply on a black/white binary; there have been Asians in America and Asian Americans for far longer than they assumed; anti-immigrant arguments have changed little over time; ordinary people have been courageously speaking back to oppression throughout the nation's history; alliance across race lines has a long history, as seen in the white merchants' supporting letter; and the twentieth- and twenty-first-century stereotype of Asian Americans as the model minority — people of color who work hard and therefore supposedly do not have to deal with racism — conveniently forgets those who have from the beginning protested anti-Asian racism.

The point here is that unless liberal humanists wish to buy into right-wing dismissal and erasure of the full scope and power of the long progressive fight for democracy in the United States and teach the young that only some groups of people care about social justice or that it is un-American to stand up as an activist, including militantly, it is important to foreground liberal activist humanities material that shows that the struggle for equity and justice in the United States has and does come from every group of people, is not over, and can and will be won.

## Fixing Shakespeare

A free bird leaps
on the back of the wind
— Maya Angelou, "Caged Bird"

Henry David Thoreau and Pauline Elizabeth Hopkins meet in John Brown. While Thoreau wrote passionately in defense of the radical abolitionist on the eve of his execution, Hopkins made him a major character in her militant 1902 novel, *Winona*. In addition, and anticipating environmental justice activists today, these two meet in their shared belief that human justice and love for the earth must not be separated.

Their lives could hardly have differed more. Thoreau graduated from Harvard and did not need to work to eat. He could reside safely alone in the woods, and he suffered little, if at all, for his outspoken, unconventional opinions, which were widely admired throughout the twentieth century and remain so today. More than a generation younger, Hopkins as an African American woman had no access to a Harvard education, and she had to earn her own way throughout her life. She could not feel safe alone in the woods, particularly at the turn into the twentieth century, the height of lynching, the legacy of which, as Evelyn White explains in "Black Women and the Wilderness," persists today. And she paid dearly for her strong opinions. Hopkins lost her position editing the *Colored American Magazine*, the major outlet for her prolific writing during her four years at the magazine, because of her outspoken criticism of Booker T. Washington. He saw her endorsement of Du Bois's views as an attack on him, which it was, and secretly bought the magazine to revamp it and remove her. Had scholars such as Henry Louis Gates, Jr., Lois Brown, and John Gruesser not made activist scholarly commitments to reissuing and discussing her writing almost a century later, we might not know of Hopkins at this time.

Yet despite such different lives, Thoreau and Hopkins stand as forebears in what we think of today as the struggle for environmental justice. Vandana Shiva explains in *Earth Democracy* that contemporary corporate globalization not only destroys local economies but also violates deep beliefs held across time and cultures that some things are not for sale, the idea that, as Shiva says: "Certain things are not tradable and will be governed by values other than commodity values" (30). Thoreau argued that point in almost everything he wrote. His anticonsumerism, reverence for nature, and adamant opposition to slavery represent a completely unified ethic that radically rejects the first principle of capitalism, the idea of ownership — of things, of the earth, of other people. He knew that disrespect for the earth and racial oppression come from the same place ideologically and morally — as did Pauline Hopkins, who opens *Winona* with a rewrite of *The Tempest* to say just that.

*WINONA* REVELS IN activism. Depicting the Underground Railroad and John Brown's militancy in Kansas, it appeared in installments in the *Colored American Magazine* at a time of such virulent antiblack racism in the United States that the turn into the twentieth century is often called the nadir of African American history. The Supreme Court legalized segregation in *Plessy v. Ferguson* in 1896; black men faced blatant disenfranchisement as they tried to vote; reparations promised freedpeople during Reconstruction were denied; and lynch mobs, often in full Ku Klux Klan regalia, terrorized and murdered African Americans with impunity.

At this time of overwhelming real-world racist violence, *Winona* begins by revising *The Tempest*. Hopkins throws out Shakespeare's fantasy of America's origin in wizardly enslavement of the dark aborigine and paternal protection of the white virgin daughter. She imagines instead a multiracial island paradise — a place between Canada and the United States but belonging to neither — where a made-up New World family dwells idyllically in the woods. The white father, adopted by Seneca people and given the name White Eagle, lives as an Indian. The mother, now dead, escaped from slavery with an orphaned boy, Judah, and after marrying White Eagle gave birth to their daughter, Winona. An old indigenous woman named Nokomis completes the group.

These four — a white man who chooses to live as an Indian, a formerly enslaved African American boy, a freeborn mixed-race girl of black and white ancestry raised in Native ways and bearing an Indian name, and an indigenous grandmother — comprise the New World family that Pauline Hopkins envisions. Clearly intended as an ideal representation of what America is not but could be, a loving multiracial family living in harmony with the land, this opening image rejects *The Tempest*. Hopkins includes all the key elements of Shakespeare's play: the island; the great white father (owning his role in Shakespeare, disowning it in Hopkins; a sorcerer in the former, a healer in the second); the missing mother; the slavery-marked black male (Caliban, subjugated; Judah, emancipated); the virginal daughter (whiter than white in Shakespeare, mixed race in Hopkins); and the out-of-the-ordinary, ultrawise, androgynous truth-speaker (Ariel, Nokomis). Hopkins's rewrite does contain problems. She romanticizes indigenous people and beliefs even as she uses racist terms such as *squaw* and *savage*. She retains a white father, making it worse rather than better by putting him in feathers. She erases Native men and kills off the black mother. Yet, problematic as it is, this opening vision attempts something hugely important: a reminder that America does not have to accept the handed-down versions of who the people are. As activist historians such as Ronald Takaki and Howard Zinn show today and William Apess said before her, Hopkins declares that the story can be retold. It is possible to reclaim and then build the future from a narrative different from the tale of arrogant European conquest imagined by Shakespeare. It is possible to tell a new story that inspires people to work for a racially inclusive United States rooted in respect for Native values and the land.

THE TEMPEST IN *Winona* is the hurricane of violence in 1850s America over the question of slavery. Specifically, it is the storm in Kansas where John Brown leads the abolitionists. Elaborately plotted (like all of Hopkins's work), the novel mixes history and fiction to praise Brown, place militant blacks and whites side by side as activists, draw obvious parallels between slaveholders before the Civil War and lynch mobs after it, and appeal directly for radical moral revolution in the United States.

In the novel a John Brown supporter on the Underground Railroad whose "eyes — his whole face, in fact — glowed and scintillated with holy wrath and conviction in the justice of his case" (350) jeers at charges that he is unpatriotic: "Treason! the word by which traitors seek to hang those who resist them. I hate the laws that make this country a nursery for slavery, and I resist them by rescuing all who come to me for refuge. . . . Oppression is oppression, whether it enslaves men and women and makes them beasts of burden, or shuts your mouth and mine if we utter humane protests against cruelty. If this is treason, make the most of it" (351). Obviously voicing her own views here, Hopkins celebrates resistance and, like every other activist writer I've discussed, indicts religion for its failure to lead: "If Christianity, Moham-medanism, or even Buddhism, did exercise the gentle and humanizing influence that is claimed for them, these horrors would cease now that actual slavery has been banished from our land" (385). She then avails herself of the jeremiad, invoking the wrath of God and prophesying a change in the fortunes of whites. They will not always be in power. How, then, Hopkins asks, will the reckoning go?

*Winona* links social justice and reverence for the environment, a con-junction of values promoted in many African American texts, as both Jeffrey Myers and Kimberly Ruffin point out. The opening of Hop-kins's novel argues that America must embrace its multiracial origins and ground the nation's values in indigenous ways of living with, not in opposition to, the earth. The narrative then confronts the historical struggle for racial equity that the abolition of slavery signified. The two together — living in harmony with the earth and fighting fiercely for racial justice — form for Hopkins one truth.

DISCUSSION OF Apess, Walker, Stowe, Thoreau, and Hopkins in my seminar Boston Radicals made me reflect on the academic writing I had assigned. Students were reading the work of activists who sought to change the minds and hearts of people for the purpose of changing the world. Yet I was asking for another footnoted paper to be read only by me, another dutiful, even if interesting, exercise in performing a critical analysis of some specific text for no particular reason except to show their professor they could do it.

We threw out the plan I walked in with and made their writing the activist component of the course. Instead of papers that only I would see, students attempted to make their voices heard in public forums. Each wrote four pieces to submit for publication in any of the university newspapers or magazines and in their hometown paper or other outlets of their choice. The goal was threefold: to provide real-world activist practice in contributing knowledge and opinions to the public discourse; to link our work in the course to questions and concerns of theirs in the present; and to honor the material we were studying by participating in the liberal tradition of writing as a crucial tool in the struggle for progressive social change.

The students produced powerful writing that, in turn, empowered them. One used *Walden* to reflect on her working-class upbringing and how she learned from her father and grandmother that life is not about material possessions. One, upon reading David Walker's *Appeal*, decided to write back to his high school paper about unaddressed racism there. One challenged peers actually to read *Uncle Tom's Cabin*. One used the contemporary poet Martín Espada as her model for writing poems in honor of her grandmother who survived a Nazi concentration camp. One used the denial of education to all but the privileged in nineteenth-century America to advocate for women's education in her homeland of Zambia today. One, after studying Apess, educated himself about the issue of Indian mascots in sports and spoke out as a white athlete against anti-Indian racism. The students wrote about the importance of voting, the human cost of global capitalism, the imperative of nonconformity, the protection of the environment, the continuing legacy of slavery, the value of religious faith, the perniciousness of religious faith, the red-white-and-blue tradition of communism in America, the erasure of Native Americans in U.S. education, the power of poetry, the pressure to consume, the right-wing toxification of the term *feminism*, and much more. They quoted material in the course, and they wrote independent of it, using it as inspiration rather than as a focus. They thought hard about audience and revised vigorously because they hoped to get published. And they did. A lot of their writing showed up in print, in some cases provoking responses, positive as well as hostile. Their writing transformed a humanities course about activist writers into one providing them with skills and practice in being activist writers.

IN SPEAKING THE TRUTH James Cone emphasizes that the way to combat violence is to create justice. People cannot expect to have nonviolence without justice, he stresses, and the point animates not just *Winona* but all of the activist texts I have talked about. Also informing them is the prophetic tradition extolled by Cornel West in *Democracy Matters*. Hopkins repeatedly refers to John Brown as a prophet and places by his side as an equal in courage and resistance her imagined black militant, Judah, whom she also calls a prophet. The move makes black activism in the fight for democracy equal with that of the most famous of the holy warriors (to use James Brewer Stewart's well-known term), John Brown, a radical admired deeply and widely from Lydia Maria Child and Frederick Douglass in his own time to W. E. B. Du Bois in Hopkins's. *Winona* links John Brown and Judah to tell a new story — as, indeed, the whole novel does, beginning with its opening vision of what America could be ecologically and racially and ending with Hopkins's giving the last word to an old enslaved woman who foresees with confidence the end of slavery. This old black woman says to an old white woman in words resonant in Hopkins's day but still prophetic in ours, "Somethin's gwine drap. White folks been ridin' a turrible hoss in this country, an' dat hoss gwine to fro 'em' you hyar me" (436). Justice will come, one way or the other.

In her "Address at the *Citizens' William Lloyd Garrison Centenary Celebration*" in December 1905 Pauline Hopkins told the gathering in Boston's historic Faneuil Hall: "Yesterday I sat in the old Joy street church and you can imagine my emotions as I remembered my great grandfather begged in England the money that helped the Negro cause, that my grandfather on my father's side, signed the papers with Garrison at Philadelphia. I remembered that at Bunker Hill my ancestors on my maternal side poured out their blood. I am a daughter of the Revolution, you do not acknowledge black daughters of the Revolution but we are going to take that right" (355). In words that apply to Hopkins but also to Apess, Walker, Stowe, Thoreau, the Chinese merchants, and the unknown authors of the early *corridos* as well as to countless other liberal activist writers in the United States, past and present, Jim Wallis observes in *God's Politics*: "The prophets always begin in judgment, in a social critique of the status quo, but they end in hope — that these realities can and will be changed" (346). Such hope is not easy or simpleminded. In *Prophetic Reflections* the interviewer says to Cornel West: "You are really preaching *hope*, I think." To which West responds: "That's it. That's right. But it is a hope that is grounded in a particular messy struggle and it is tarnished by any kind of naive projections of a better future, *so that it is hope on the tight rope* rather than a Utopian projection that looks over and beyond the present and oftentimes loses sight of the present" (67). Hope, as West says, on the tightrope.

We are living in a period of great fear and pain. Today we are deluged with more images of suffering than any previous generation: war, natural disasters, famine, poverty, and disease are beamed nightly into our living rooms. . . . It is tempting to retreat from this ubiquitous horror, to deny that it has anything to do with us, and to cultivate a deliberately "positive" attitude that excludes anybody's pain but our own.
—Karen Armstrong, *The Great Transformation*

# THREE

## The Multicultural Imperative

At an academic lecture on Asian American literature that I recently attended, an audience member asked the speaker why he didn't place quotation marks around the word *race*. Didn't his failure to use quotation marks simply support the erroneous idea that race is real? Was he asking us to fall back into "pre-post-race thinking"? The speaker responded eagerly and immediately. Yes, yes, quotation marks, of course. He certainly did not mean to suggest we should be thinking in terms of identity politics. A few weeks later a Ph.D. student shared with me her excellent ideas about the dissertation she plans to write on Asian American and African texts. But don't worry, she hastily added, I'll be critiquing multiculturalism.

Any early-twenty-first-century discussion of activism and American literature has to take into account both of these issues: the contemporary liberal disavowal of race and the contemporary liberal denigration of multiculturalism. Both undercut the activist struggle for progressive change.

## The Postrace Hoax

I'm marked by the color of my skin.
The bullets are discrete and designed to kill slowly.
They are aiming at my children.
These are facts.
— Lorna Dee Cervantes, *Emplumada*

Current academic theory explains that many categories previously considered natural, even biological, and therefore presumably universal and fixed, such as gender, race, and sexuality, are in fact social constructions. They are invented human concepts that change greatly across time and cultures, do not have provable bases in biology, and exist to perpetuate specific systems of power such as patriarchy, white supremacy, and enforced heterosexuality.

In the case of race, the issue at the heart of multiculturalism, social construction theory shows that we are not talking about a biological category. Western science has attempted for more than 150 years to establish race as a biological fact. It has placed human hair under a microscope, measured skulls, compared genitals, and diagrammed facial features. This quest continues today with DNA research in particular. But as scholars such as Howard Winant, Karen Brodkin, Ian Haney López, Ruth Frankenberg, and Joan Ferrante and Prince Browne, Jr., among others, explain, the effort to prove race as biology has itself proved impossible. No one characteristic defining a given race can be claimed;

no boundary marking where one race ends and another begins can be identified; no race gene is known; variations within a group are as big as or bigger than between groups; people of different races can reproduce; what is considered a race varies widely, even wildly, over time; and the methods of classification differ radically from group to group.

Because U.S. culture insists on race so adamantly, most people still think of race as biology. But what skin color or hair texture (or any other marker) defines African Americans? What race category designates the child of an Asian parent and a white parent? Why are Jews, Italians, or the Irish considered people of color in one era but not in another? Why categorize by drops of blood historically for blacks, enrollment lists for indigenous people, and language for Latinos? Social construction theory clearly demonstrates that race is just an idea: a human invention, a fiction, an illusion. This area of postmodern thought enables us to dismantle essentialist definitions and expose the political agendas involved in their conception and enforcement. The breakthrough has been liberating. Race as an inherent, indelible, biological fact is gone.

Yet here, too often, much liberal thinking on the subject stops, declaring that we now live in a postrace world. In particular, this occurs in the humanities, where social construction theory frequently slides into assertions that race is nothing but an idea. This is the postrace hoax. For we do not live in a postrace world — or a postgender, postnational, postcolonial, postheterosexual one either, for that matter, as even the most cursory look around makes obvious. As I write in the United States at a time when the National Urban League points out that 50 percent of African American students in 2009 will not graduate from high school, when citizens argue about whether to build a wall to keep Mexicans out, and when the *Boston Globe* in 2008 reports racial targeting of black students at Harvard by campus police and the near-fatal beating of a young black man, Tizaya Robinson, by whites in Marshfield, Massachusetts — and my state is no different from any other in the nation — it seems bizarre, to put it mildly, for intelligent people to be claiming that we have arrived at some postrace location. A publication as bland and mainstream as *USA Today* reported on 28 February 2008 that Hispanics were twice as likely to live in poverty as whites and blacks more than three times as likely. Not even mentioned were Native Americans, who are as a group most impoverished of all. For over twenty-five years *Intelligence Report*, the magazine published by the Southern Poverty Law Center, has been chronicling hate crimes in the United States, and its reporting continues today. Race and racism are *not* mere ideas in the world outside — or for many people inside — academia.

The problem comes from liberal thought within and beyond academic settings absorbing only half of the definition of race offered by social construction theory outside the humanities. Sociologists of race and critical race theorists in the field of law agree that race is not biology but emphasize at the same time that it *is* real. Race does exist. Just because it is humanly invented does not mean it does not exist or that it no longer exerts powerful influence in the world. As Joan Ferrante and Prince Browne, Jr., put it succinctly, "*Biological race* is the illusion; *social race* is not" (121). Race *is* simply an idea, a fiction, a myth. But it is *also* a social fact with real-life consequences. It is an experiential reality that carries with it lived meanings and impacts for everyone in the society.

To try to capture that paradox — race is both a fiction and a reality — a colleague and I in a team-taught course on race developed the following short definition drawing on theorists such as those I've mentioned. We explained that race is a historically shifting, socially constructed human classification system that exists to establish power. It groups people primarily by physical appearance or markers but also by other means such as ancestry, history, or language in order to advantage the dominant group (in the United States, white people) and disadvantage others (in the United States, people of color). It is the basic building block of the system of racism in the United States — the disadvantaging of people of color for the purpose of benefiting whites. This system structures and has always structured the nation.

Postrace thinking grasps the idea that race is not biology but misses the fact that it is nevertheless very real. In *The Trouble with Diversity*, for instance, humanities scholar Walter Benn Michaels criticizes benighted attachment to the notion of race despite "scientific skepticism about whether there is any such thing" (5). Not race but class, he argues, needs to be the issue. However, it makes no sense to pit these issues against each other. As many people point out, we all live class through race and gender, and gender through race and class, and so forth. Each affects our lives, and each operates through and with the others. Arguing race away does not make it disappear. In fact, as Rey Chow observes of academic debates on the subject, cultural studies' insistence on the importance of both race and class threatens poststructuralist thinking precisely because it forces elite theorists "to confront the significance of race — and with it the histories of racial discrimination and racial exploitation — that is repressed in poststructuralist theory's claim to subversiveness and radicalness" (5). Race operates in the world whether or not erudite academic theory accepts that fact. And these questions do need to be asked. Who labels race nothing but an illusion? Who is in a position to deny its reality, and who is not? Who benefits from the denial?

To erase race by saying we live in a postrace world is simply the newest and most fashionable version of color blindness, a standpoint adopted by well-meaning people that functions, ironically, as a form of racism. For when someone says, "I don't care if a person is red or white or black or green or purple," we know we have entered la-la land. There are no green or purple people. Likewise, there is no postrace America. In theory there might be, but in fact there is not. In the 2008 presidential primaries Hillary Clinton could point vociferously to the glass ceiling limiting women's advancement, while Barack Obama could not even hint at the barred and booby-trapped front door facing most black men in the United States. If anything, race remains even more highly charged than gender in the United States, and neither has arrived at anything near "post" status. A white woman or a man of color in a high position of power is acceptable to the degree that the person imitates existing white male models, a truth that only multiplies for women of color.

Color blindness is problematic because, whether motivated by old-fashioned liberal politeness or by new-fashioned liberal postracialism, it deals in power evasion. It fails to understand, or perhaps refuses to acknowledge, that race encodes power differentials and therefore does matter. To claim not to see race or that it is just a fiction is both disingenuous — people are taught in the United States, obsessively, from childhood on to see and recognize the meanings of race — and dismissive of the fact that racism affects the lives of every person in positive or negative ways. In the United States there is no place outside the system of racism. We are all in it, which means we can go along with it or we can oppose it. Opposition requires recognizing race as a *social fact* in order to take an activist stand against racism.

STUDENTS FEAR TALKING about race. Often they express this fear as displeasure with political correctness. But political correctness does not really seem to be the issue. Being politically correct in the United States early in the twenty-first century means opposing racism, and, on a spectrum of mild to passionate, my students do. What holds most of them back is fear of their own ignorance, the knowledge that they are ill equipped to deal with the subject and will, in all likelihood, quickly find themselves embarrassed, hurt, or angry. Others fear being upset by what they will hear and/or by the expectation that they will be asked to be authorities. All of them realize that experiential knowledge gives people different degrees of accuracy and depth in their awareness about race in the contemporary world. They know they will diverge greatly when it comes to what they have learned in school, at home, and in their day-to-day lives, often but not always depending on their racial identity location. Conversations in mixed-race classrooms in the past have shown them all that turbulence can easily erupt, and, understandably, most would rather avoid the whole topic than risk painful encounters.

The solution is for teachers to provide tools. Because they have not been taught, most people have extremely limited vocabularies about race and do not understand it as a system of power relations. Further, they don't see whiteness as a raced category within that system or know how racism as a system operates once we move beyond Klan members scrawling swastikas on a storefront. Yet all of these things can be learned, and excellent resources exist. In my own courses I routinely incorporate units on racism and antiracist activism, including how to form coalitions. I use material by Peggy McIntosh about white privilege, Gloria Yamato about forms of racism, Wendy Rose about anti-Indian racism in particular, and Howard Winant about race as a social construction. As students begin to develop a lexicon that allows them to discuss racism beyond a vague, gut-level awareness and share an analytical framework, they gain confidence. They start to speak with more precision and sophistication, referring, for example, to internal colonialism, unearned white advantage, aware/overt racism, aware/covert racism, unaware/unintentional racism, unaware/self-righteous racism, internalized oppression, institutional racism, honorary whiteness, the myth of the model minority, conferred dominance, and color blindness.

Psychological theory outside the humanities emphasizes that, because race is such a highly charged topic in the United States, it is very important for people to be able to reflect on where they are emotionally on the subject, as Beverly Daniel Tatum explains in "Talking about Race, Learning about Racism." Tatum lays out the standard stages of racial identity development for both white people and African Americans, which can be extended with a few modifications to all people of color; and because her presentation includes young people's statements about their experiences, I often ask students to read it and think about themselves. For most, it is extremely helpful to see that their strong feelings — anger, fear, shock, guilt, impatience, despair, shame, exhaustion — fall within a developmental model and that they are not doomed to stay stuck forever in a place that is debilitating or depressing. Racial identity development theory shows that change and growth are possible and come with increased knowledge. That awareness can mitigate the sense of hopelessness that many people have when it comes to anti-racist activism.

## Diversity Matters

We live in a multicultural society. This is not something we're striving for; it already is our reality. — Paul Kivel, *Uprooting Racism*

The world has changed. In the United States cultural material is available from a range of perspectives unimaginable thirty years ago. If you wish to explore American literature, for instance, you have a huge field to choose from. You can read fiction by the early-twentieth-century writer thought to be the first Asian North American to publish stories about Chinese America, Sui Sin Far. You can read a volume of short stories by the early-twentieth-century Mexican American writer María Cristina Mena. You can read two books by the Lakota author and activist writing at that time as well, Zitkala-Ša. You can find with no problem all of the published work of Pauline Hopkins. Twenty-five years ago each of these was available only on microfilm or in obscure, out-of-print originals. Today, however, we can think about entire literary traditions that were not even recognized as traditions years ago: Native American, Latino/a, Asian American, nineteenth-century African American, Arab American. Abundant criticism and scholarship exist to help people learn about previously excluded authors. There are volumes of essays on women writers, collections about Native American writers, shelves on Asian American texts, an entire Oxford University Press series devoted to nineteenth-century black women writers, and countless multi-racially focused critical books. Major presses — Macmillan, Bedford/ St. Martin's, Norton, Random House — now offer rich multicultural anthologies. The landscape of American literature has changed dramatically since the mid-twentieth century. We can at last understand U.S. literature from its beginnings as genuinely multiracial and therefore engage the foundational national issue of race along its many axes — not just black/white — as students, teachers, and citizens.

Yet at precisely this point many professional humanists pronounce race a false concept, and the political Right and Left unite in dismissing multiculturalism as either bad or misguided. This backlash is not simply regrettable, it is dangerous. Not to understand the United States as multiracial — in the common terminology, multicultural — is to reaffirm the ideology of white supremacy that the nation is founded on, continues to operate in terms of, and has, along with Europe, exported to the rest of the world, with disastrous results. Committing to multiculturalism is not optional. It is imperative if human beings are to achieve social justice and planetary health, for both depend upon recognizing the role of race and racism as systems of power in the constitution of a world that desperately needs reconstitution.

WHY IS multiculturalism under attack?

Multiculturalism is about radical change. It is not about food festival diversity — tasting a little bit of this culture and a little bit of that, singing kumbaya, and saying oh what a wonderful society. It's not, as Richard Dyer explains white people in particular too often believe, simply a delightful sideshow, one more consumable display of how fascinating and exotic people of color are presumed to be. Nor is it about tokenism, sticking Rosa Parks or Martin Luther King, Jr., always *the* additions, into otherwise all-white paradigms. And it is not about hiring one or two people of color to do the work of creating change while white people continue with business as usual, as Shirley Geok-lin Lim, María Herrera-Sobek, and Genara Padilla point out. Further, it insists on white people as a raced group. It does not remove them from the picture and thus, whether implicitly or explicitly, from the system of race and racism. Multiculturalism is about *all* areas not identified as race or ethnicity specific, such as African American literature or Irish American social clubs, having a genuinely multiracial focus and informed explicit attention to racism as part of their awareness.

This is not anything new.

Multiculturalism originated in the United States in the liberatory struggles of the 1960s and 1970s: the black civil rights movement, the second wave of feminism, the American Indian Movement, the Chicano rights struggle, antiwar activism, Asian American resistance to racism, and the gay rights movement. It began as an overtly political project inside and outside the academy committed to respect for and, at the very least, full and representative inclusion of people of color, white women, and gay and lesbian people as equals in the telling of the nation's story (history, literature), laws made and enforced (politics, government), business conducted (the workplace), news reported (media), and services rendered (medicine, education). Multiculturalism as an attack on white patriarchal dominance understood itself as a liberation movement grounded in identity politics, the belief that a person's gender, race, class, and sexual orientation make a difference in what that person knows and experiences in the society and therefore how he or she affiliates politically. As an antiracist movement at its core, multiculturalism reasoned: if the environment — cultural and literal — is no longer only or uncontestedly white, the justice claims and interests of people of color can gain broad influence, and that will lead to significant antiracist change.

This original multicultural agenda, needless to say, has not been realized. First, racial inclusivity has not occurred at any level. In the field of literature, for example, the percentages of people of color teaching in secondary and postsecondary English departments remain extremely low. Nor has curriculum undergone major transformation. I canvass my students, graduate as well as undergraduate. Can they list five Native American writers? Or Asian American? Or Latino/a? What is the Dawe's Land Allotment Act? The Chinese Exclusion Act? The amount of Mexico confiscated in the Treaty of Guadalupe Hidalgo? Beyond a little knowledge about African American literature and history, not much has changed for my students. And what they do know about progressive human rights struggle in the United States remains minuscule.

Second and simultaneously, multiculturalism *has* been lapped up by global capitalism. Glossy images of prosperous perfect people of color adorn buses, billboards, TV ads, and multinational corporations' annual reports. Benetton. Coca Cola. Halliburton. Multiculturalism has become the marketing mantra of übercapitalism. One completely legitimate criticism of multiculturalism holds that the corporate world exploits the idea of racial diversity to line the pockets of the rich. Very true.

Third, right-wing propaganda labels both the term and the concept a threat to the nation. "The costs of multiculturalism — in terms of disunity, the clash of classes, and declining trust — are likely to be huge in the long run," the director of an institute at a prestigious law school, Lawrence Harrison, warns. "All cultures are not equal when it comes to promoting progress, and very few can match Anglo-Protestantism in this respect. We should be promoting acculturation to the national mainstream, not a mythical, utopian multiculturalism." Similarly, Matthew Spalding charges in the Heritage Foundation magazine, the *Insider,* that multiculturalism undermines "the very idea of allegiance, especially national or patriotic." Only assimilation "prevents the American 'melting pot' from becoming a boiling cauldron of multiculturalism" (20, 21), he cautions.

Fourth, various thinkers on the left reject multiculturalism. Many postmodernists, like their neoconservative counterparts on the political right, dismiss it — often with contempt or at the very least an impatient expression of shock that someone could still be espousing such a discredited idea. Since the foundational concept of multiculturalism is race, and race is an illusion, then multiculturalism is based on nothing, or worse: illegitimate essentialist thinking. Others emphasize multi-culturalism's co-optation by consumer culture. For them, its degeneration into feel-good diversity emptied of all attention to racism or other power dynamics has so weakened the concept that it is no longer useful. Still others on the left such as Todd Gitlin and Michael Tomasky attack multiculturalism for taking attention away from class.

So this is where we are now. Global capitalism uses multiculturalism as a sales tool. The political Right declares multiculturalism un-American. And the political Left, especially in the academy, has for the most part either abandoned the concept as intellectually corrupt or joined the Right in branding it divisive.

BUT MULTICULTURALISM is crucial to progressive change in the United States. In *Playing in the Dark* Toni Morrison explains that there is no such thing as unraced or raceless space in the national imaginary. She points out that the United States is "a wholly racialized society" (12–13). Race and racism saturate every aspect of American life. Consequently, Morrison explains of the area she knows best, *all* American literature engages in an "encounter with racial ideology. American literature could not help being shaped by that encounter" (16). She notes especially the Africanist presence in white-authored texts, the impossibility of keeping blackness out if the subject is America. But I quote her statement that the United States is a wholly racialized society to emphasize the fact that the nation is and always has been multiracial. That is what I mean by the multicultural imperative. If progressive people in the United States are serious about working for meaningful social change that involves and respects all people, including young people who already know that it is not just national but global multiraciality that has to be comprehended, then liberal thinkers must recommit to and act upon the truth that both the nation and the world are profoundly multicultural and that multiculturalism represents a politically crucial value.

Multiculturalism does present challenges. In the study of American literature, for instance, which has typically been defined as white, what does change mean? After adding *Invisible Man* or *Their Eyes Were Watching God*, then what? What Native American texts? What Latino ones? Asian American? And few people can even name Arab American possibilities, despite events in the world for the past two decades. How do teachers help students understand unfamiliar work, especially if it falls outside the teacher's cultural comfort zone? And what about classics that won't get taught? Replace *Sister Carrie* with *Mrs. Spring Fragrance*? Ernest Hemingway with Jean Toomer? Willa Cather with Zitkala-Ša? What happens to beloved paradigms? The American Renaissance. The closing of the frontier.

These are not small or foolish concerns. Lack of knowledge, worry about tradition, loss of beloved texts and paradigms: all are real and understandable issues. It is important to admit the truth. *The multicultural imperative does involve radical change.* It is about transformation. It requires alteration of what people know and value. In every area it means redefining organizing concepts, committing to environments in which white voices do not dominate, and going beyond a black/white paradigm, since the United States is not and never has been only a black/white place. The multicultural imperative means regarding white points of view as raced points of view — points of view that are not neutral but are, in a racist society such as the United States, inevitably every bit as affected by race and racism as points of view of people of color. Certainly it means learning how to understand and talk about race and racism as systems of power and working hard to end racism.

In *Earth Democracy* Vandana Shiva outlines ten principles for justice, sustainability, and peace in the world. Number three is: *diversity in nature and culture must be defended.* The contemporary world is beginning to recognize the truth of the first half of this principle, which earth-based societies have always known. Life depends on biodiversity. Healthy oceans, soils, plants, air, and animals all require maintenance and preservation of diversity. Imbalance caused by one element becoming dominant and taking over destroys the health of the entire ecosystem. So, too, racism, in the form of white dominance in the United States and colonialism around the world, destroys the health of societies. It creates severe imbalance that eventually collapses of its own weight or will explode from below when the gap between dominator and dominated grows intolerable to those unjustly subordinated. David Walker prophesied that truth in 1830. Leslie Marmon Silko and Karen Tei Yamashita reiterate it in our time, as I turn to in my last chapter. Commitment to multiculturalism as a national and global principle is about the health and survival of the world. Peace depends not upon dominance and force but upon people respecting each other as equals across lines of difference. That means, among other things, that no one group such as whites can continue to hoard disproportionate wealth and power at the expense of people of color nationally and around the globe.

MULTICULTURALISM CAN present itself as simply celebratory — delight in diversity. That's fine but finally of little importance. The multicultural imperative is about diversity that includes a clear power analysis of the system of racism that functions to create and maintain advantage and disadvantage. For that reason, knowledge coming from members of subordinated groups counts particularly heavily because their social locations, structurally, allow for strong insight into how power operates in the world. That is why Satya Mohanty says multiculturalism inside and outside the academy must foreground perspectives of people in subordinated groups to generate objective knowledge. Without such bottom-up perspectives, he explains, there is no way to gain a full or accurate picture of reality.

A good example is the late-nineteenth- and early-twentieth-century literary period in the United States known as American Realism, which contains work by well-known authors such as Mark Twain, Henry James, Stephen Crane, Upton Sinclair, and William Dean Howells. Except for James, each of these white men used his writing to advocate for progressive social change. Crane, Sinclair, Howells, and Twain did so quite overtly. They also, except for James, took strong, liberal stands on public issues. Twain, for instance, inveighed against U.S. military imperialism in the Spanish American War. Howells bitterly condemned the U.S. government's execution of political leftists following the Haymarket Square riots and used his editorial prestige to support African American writers. Upton Sinclair relentlessly attacked the exploitation of workers by unregulated industrial capitalism. The work of these men, except for James, is extremely important in the liberal activist tradition in U.S. literature.

But we could read every book ever written by Twain, Crane, Sinclair, and Howells and still have only a very partial view of the liberal activist tradition. The white feminist anger of Charlotte Perkins Gilman in *The Yellow Wallpaper,* which shows the severe psychic pain suffered by many women in traditional marriages, comes directly from a woman. The righteous black anger of W. E. B. Du Bois in *The Souls of Black Folk,* which maps the white racist destruction of Reconstruction, or of

Charles Chesnutt in *The Marrow of Tradition,* which presents the terrible Wilmington race riots from an African American point of view, can only be found in such black-authored texts. The exposé of anti-Asian racism by Sui Sin Far in *Mrs. Spring Fragrance,* which chronicles the lethal impact of U.S. immigration policies on Chinese people forced into detention camps, cannot be found in white-authored work at the time. Nor can even the most liberal dominant-culture texts of the period provide the same scathing indictment of U.S. imperialism as stories by María Cristina Mena such as "The Education of Popo," which quite deliberately rewrites Henry James's *Daisy Miller* from the point of view of the colonized native rather than the rich white tourists. And nothing in any of these works, whether by white writers or writers of color who are not indigenous, even begins to speak to the issues of anti-Indian racism and indigenous resistance, including refusal to give up Native religious beliefs, articulated by Zitkala-Ša in *Old Indian Legends* and *American Indian Stories.*

Progressive activists need all of these perspectives. But especially important are those of underrepresented populations. For as Paula Moya reminds us, "the culture of power must make its dominance appear natural — must convince everyone that what is, is what should be. That is why the alternative perspectives of members of subordinated cultures within a larger society will have the potential to teach all of us more about the relations of power in a society than the perspectives of the members of the dominant culture in that same society" (169). Sharing that outlook, John Wills emphasizes that multiculturalism is needed by everyone — whites as well as people of color — not because it's nice or politically correct but because it is the lifeblood of democracy and the basis for progressive change in a multiracial world.

## What's at Stake?

Like an individual, America can be whole only by going back to its roots —
all of them. — Marilou Awiakta, *Selu*

A few years ago a friend decided to begin her class on nineteenth-
century American literature with a screening of the 1915 racist film, *The
Birth of a Nation*. Based on a best-selling novel and used as a Ku Klux
Klan recruiting tool, it would do an excellent job, she believed, of re-
vealing how blatant and full of lies antiblack racism was at the end of the
century students were about to study. When the film ended, a young
white woman stopped to thank the professor, who is African American,
for showing it. The student explained that she had never known why
the Klan was formed, but now — to my friend's horror — she understood why it was needed.

*The Birth of a Nation* remains so potent today because its basic racist
story of imperiled whiteness is still with us. In fact, the film includes
almost every major racist narrative still current in the United States. In
addition to overtly demeaning African Americans, it orientalizes the
mistress of a main character and invokes anti-Muslim vitriol by cos-
tuming the Klansmen (plus their horses) as Crusaders. It labels white
antiracists fools and traitors and, in its climactic scene, triumphantly
echoes the anti-Indian racism of Buffalo Bill Cody's enormously popular Wild West Show. The film shows a log cabin surrounded by blood-
thirsty savages, whom, in the nick of time, the Klan (aka the cavalry)
charges in to slaughter.

My own students, even though I have them view *The Birth of a Nation* midway through the semester and after considerable preparation (I
am grateful for my friend's advice), find themselves shocked by its impact. They despise its racism and audibly gasp when this subtitle flashes

on the screen: *"North and South unite in common defense of their Aryan birthright."* People in the United States actually used the language they associate only with Hitler? The film was shown in the White House, and President Wilson praised it lavishly? They find it hard to believe. Nevertheless, many of them are appalled to discover themselves successfully manipulated into rooting for the Klan at key moments. The Wagnerian musical score and white-damsel-in-distress plot suck them in. But then the film's final image of the Ultimate Klansman jolts them. In flowing white robes and blond-haired, blue-eyed, Aryan splendor, Jesus appears in the sky as the "Star-Spangled Banner" plays and beatific white heterosexual couples marry. This crude collapse of white power, enforced heterosexuality, and Christianity into one patriotic hymn to hatred almost makes them laugh. Until someone asks if anyone else noticed how much *King Kong* — or some other popular movie — mimics the basic story line of *The Birth of a Nation.*

HISTORICALLY, the movie was the film industry's first big blockbuster. Although it opened elsewhere, *The Birth of a Nation* played in New York City in March 1915 under enormous billboards of Klansmen in full regalia to advertise the event. Actors on horseback in KKK robes rode through city streets to promote it; and across the country tens of thousands of people lined up to see the three-hour-long epic. For many, as was the case with my own parents, who were poor and still children at the time, it was their first moving picture, and it made an indelible, destructive impression. Long before I saw the movie my father and mother recommended it as realism (which it is not). But the film also generated adamant protest from the outset, especially from the NAACP, founded six years before its debut. The film's maker, D. W. Griffith, famously stated, "I believe in the motion picture not only as a means of amusement but also as a moral and educational force," and activists responded by picketing theaters and blasting the movie's racism in print. The African American poet and novelist James Weldon Johnson, author of the song known as the black national anthem, "Lift Every Voice and Sing," attacked the press for its "utter stupidity" in claiming not to understand why the film provoked "resentment among colored people and fair-minded white people" (156). Johnson — like others — took a stand immediately against the film's racism and misrepresentation of facts.

*The Birth of a Nation* is one of the urtexts of U.S. racism. Ideologically, artistically, commercially, politically: in every way, as Clyde Taylor explains and DJ Spooky's edited version today makes clear, it lays out the foundational narrative of white supremacy that antiracists have for more than two centuries now resisted. Multiculturalism is about that resistance — past, present, and future — *and* about the alternative vision of an inclusive and democratic society that antiracist activism seeks to make reality.

TO THE OBJECTION that real change will never occur, I am reminded of my own experience. Three and a half decades ago, in seven years of undergraduate and graduate coursework at three different institutions, I had no professor who was a person of color and only one who was a woman. I read no literature by writers of color and, except for Emily Dickinson, no woman writer until my last semester of graduate school, when I took a class taught by, it will come as no surprise, that one white woman. Today a postsecondary English department in the United States without women faculty and with an all-male or almost-all-male curriculum would be hard to find. The same is true outside academic settings. Women today manage banks and own businesses. Although not as well represented as they should be, they hold elected offices, and they work prominently in the media. Similarly, it can be said of gay and lesbian rights that, although much remains to accomplish, tremendous progress has been made. In the United States same-sex marriage, although still under threat, has become law in several states. Movies and television programs treat gay issues openly, and more and more workplace and social situations reject the kind of antigay hatred that few heterosexual people even blinked at as recently as the early 1990s. Likewise, as many people point out with justification, something important has shifted with regard to racism in the United States if a black man can be elected as president. The point is this: change does happen. Misogyny, homophobia, and racism are hardly extinct. Backlash can be explosive — and highly destructive, as racist attacks on President Obama and revocation of same-sex marriage in California, for instance, indicate. But progress does occur.

Still, major questions persist. Will communities of color in the United States renounce homophobia as a violation of basic human rights no less damaging than racism and then confront it within their own ranks? Will the many white women and gays and lesbians who are the direct beneficiaries of the women's movement and the gay rights struggle of the 1960s and 1970s *but also* of the civil rights struggle of that same era, white people who have benefited tremendously and disproportionately from the fight for affirmative action and human rights led by people of color, embrace or abandon fundamental antiracist social change? Will all these groups work together for the common good? Will they, above all, unite in addressing the overriding issue of our own time of looming ecological ruin that is already devastating the world's poor, who constitute most of the earth's population and the overwhelming majority of whom are people of color?

The resurgence of interest in modernism among academic humanists may not augur well. As Paul Lauter argues in *From Walden Pond to Jurassic Park*, high modernism valorizes hyperindividualism, alienation, and disaffection. It relishes an aesthetic of deliberate difficulty and elite erudition, privileging angst and exclusivity over belief in the power of ordinary people to come together to create progressive social change. We live in a time of retreat among professional humanists into increasingly conservative, socially disengaged positions that close out the majority of people and mistake rhetoric for action. Skepticism and endless critical thinking for its own sake have become goods in and of themselves, while the power of the humanities to teach us how to change the world for the better gets lost. Fredric Jameson cautions in *Postmodernism, or, The Cultural Logic of Late Capitalism* that "Left cultural producers and theorists . . . have often by reaction allowed themselves to be unduly intimidated by the repudiation, in bourgeois aesthetics and most notably in high modernism, of one of the age-old functions of art — the pedagogical and the didactic" (50). Cornel West worried about this in relation to the study of African American literature almost two decades ago, arguing in *Keeping the Faith* that a preference for introspection and a dehydrating emphasis on the professionalization of literary criticism were depoliticizing black studies.

Some attacks on multiculturalism from the Left charge that identity politics undermine the radical humanism begun by the Enlightenment, the discourse of universal rights and liberty that emerged in eighteenth-century Europe and formed the basis for both the American and the French revolutions. In this view the agendas of feminists, people of color, and gays and lesbians divide what would otherwise be a unified Left concentration on class struggle. In response, Robin D. G. Kelley points out that the so-called universal rights discourse of the Enlightenment never applied to the majority of people. From the beginning it went hand in hand with enslavement of Africans, genocide against indigenous people in the Americas, and subjugation of women. Kelley suggests that the real problem might be that "the neo-Enlightenment Left cannot conceive of movements led by African Americans, women, Latinos, or gays and lesbians speaking for the whole or even embracing radical humanism" (108). Kelley turns the tables and argues that identity politics actually offers the basis for our all coming together *as* radical humanists to work for fundamental change.

WHITE RACISM, Kelley observes, has destroyed most progressive movements in the United States. For contemporary liberal activists in the United States, that point cannot be overemphasized. Multiculturalism challenges white people in particular to recognize that whites as a group in the United States and around the world by birthright hold illegitimate conferred power. Also, it challenges whites who do recognize that fact to position themselves as colleagues and allies rather than bosses in the struggle for justice led by people of color. To a large extent, the white response in the United States from both the Left and the Right has been to deal with these realities by trying to reclaim the center through attacking multiculturalism as passé (the Left) or seditious (the Right) and identity politics as essentialist (the Left) or unpatriotic (the Right). Progressive people need to recognize that both avenues of attack conveniently reinforce white power by keeping white supremacy in place, whether people intend that or not.

Paula Moya and others courageously defend identity politics. Moya acknowledges that Chicana as a postmodern concept of detached oppositionality is useful politically. But she goes on to advocate the recuperative theory known as postpositive realism because all of our identities —

even if shifting and complex — are also very real. She maintains that "it is only when we have a realist account of our identities, one that refers outward to the world we live in, will we be able to understand what social and political possibilities are open to us for the purpose of working to build a better society" (99).

It is this last phrase I wish to underscore: *for the purpose of working to build a better society*. That is why diversity matters. Detached from clear analysis of power relations and explicit dedication to antiracist activism, multiculturalism means nothing. Paul Kivel points out, as my epigraph states, that society is already multicultural. What it is not and has never been, Kivel emphasizes, is democratic and antiracist. For that reason, he says the only worthwhile multiculturalism is what he labels "democratic, anti-racist multiculturalism" (223). He is right.

Here is what is at stake in repudiating the postrace hoax — the idea that we live in a postrace world — and embracing the multicultural imperative — creation of a social order that is genuinely inclusive and antiracist: recommitment to social justice as the foundational, urgent question invigorating humanist thought everywhere. The persistent hegemonic narrative of "America" is and always has been white supremacy, and that ideology remains one of the nation's major exports to every corner of the globe. Not to understand the United States, past and present, multiculturally is not neutral. It is endorsement of that hegemonic narrative of white supremacy.

One of my undergraduate students wrote in her journal a year ago:

I was struck the other day in class when you questioned us about when the last time was in our education that we learned about Native American cultures. I can't remember learning a thing about Native Americans except in relation to the Thanksgiving story and some early United States History. Even in the History class though, the focus certainly wasn't on Native Americans, but rather on how we acquisitioned our land. . . . I have never read a book by a Native American author. This made me think. . . . Yet, how many countless books have I read by [white] American and European Authors? Countless.

Who decides what literature is worth reading to our children and in our schools? How does that affect the existing racial and cultural situation in the United States?

How indeed?

Again and again, it was necessary to
remind everyone that no education is
politically neutral.
—bell hooks, *Teaching to Transgress*

# FOUR

## Rising Waters

In *The Souls of Black Folk* in 1903 W. E. B. Du Bois prophesied that the problem of the twentieth century was the problem of the color line. It does not take a prophet today to predict that the problem of the twenty-first century is the problem of ecological disaster.

Five centuries of Western colonialism, capitalism, enforced Christianity, racism, systematic sexism, and ever-more-sophisticated warfare have brought the globe to a perilous brink. Soil depletion so destroyed agriculture in Haiti even pre-2010 that street vendors in Port-au-Prince sell pies made of clay, salt, and shortening as food. Arctic ice melts and with it the habitat of bears who have lived there for millennia. Life expectancy for an indigenous person on the Wind River Reservation in the United States of America is forty-nine years. Worldwide desertification now consumes an area larger than Canada and the United States combined. As I write, human disconnect from and disrespect for the earth — the much-vaunted Western ideology of endless, unlimited, burgeoning capitalism, now riding high globally, an ethic of constant consumption, advance, and accumulation — fattens a minuscule portion of the earth's people while it starves the vast majority, destroys entire ecosystems, burns a hole in the ozone, and drives species into extinction. As George Monbiot explains in *Heat*, the United States needs to cut carbon emissions by 90 percent by 2030 in order to avert irreversible global catastrophe.

Many of my students know and fear these truths. Others try not to know out of feelings of despair and powerlessness. What can any one person or even group of people possibly do to halt, much less reverse, devastation of such magnitude? Still others cling to technology. Maybe we can somehow invent ourselves out of the looming crisis. Cars that do not pollute. Food from some imaginary inexhaustible fields not affected by climate change or the soil erosion that results from economic imperialism forcing poor people around the globe to deforest their own land. Perhaps there will be satellites in space where human beings can live after the earth has burnt to a cinder. Science will have answers.

Deep in our hearts, however, we know that science and technology do not have the answer. The crisis is one of values. It can be met, like the problem Du Bois spoke of one hundred years ago, only by a radical shift in belief, a profound realignment of thought and spirit.

The basic principle is simple and earth based. All human beings must come to understand ourselves as living in relationship with — not in opposition to or mastery of — the earth and all of our fellow beings, human and not human. It is what Awiakta explains in *Selu* as the law of respect: the fundamental Cherokee truth that you must give back when you take from the earth. You cannot take, take, take and not expect disaster to occur. Life exists within a circle or cycle of interconnected taking and giving, a web of interdependence. Michael Lerner, speaking of contemporary spiritual feminism's perspective on human relations, refers to this as the mandate to "see each individual woman and man as part of the unity of all being, as fundamentally interconnected, and each decision we make as one that emanates from our link to all others, having consequences that will affect all others" (268). This principle of interconnection extends to all life, social and environmental. As Awiakta states of the law of respect, "The sacred law is eternal and immutable. You must take and give back with respect" (30). Everyone knows that to remove, raid, or eliminate one element in an ecosystem throws the health of the whole system into crisis and, often, extinction. Yet contemporary corporate globalization constantly performs precisely those acts of raid and depletion daily. To enrich the few, it exploits and impoverishes the majority and plunges the earth's balance into chaos. The disastrous effects are already felt by huge numbers of people, animals, and plants and will soon catch up with all of us.

Environmental justice as an activist movement focuses on the disproportionate environmental harm experienced by people of color and poor whites so that the privileged few can enjoy health and inordinate wealth. Environmentalism as a movement concerns itself with protection of the natural world. It concentrates on such things as land conservation, endangered species, and aesthetic and recreational issues such as parks and open space. In contrast, the fight for social justice concerns itself with human inequity. It focuses on discrimination based on race, class, gender, sexuality, nationality, religion, and/or physical ability. Environmental justice brings these two areas of progressive struggle together. It yokes concern about the environment to the fight for human rights and equity, with particular attention to the intersection where environmental abuse and human targeting meet.

To help students grasp the concept in my course titled Environmental Justice and U.S. Literature, I ask some questions on the first day. What happens to your trash when you throw it out? In which part of the city are asthma rates highest? Where does radioactive uranium waste go? To what South American country does the United States ship highly polluting old New England manufacturing plants for reassembly and use? What is the cancer rate among the migrant workers who picked the fruits and vegetables you ate in the university dining halls today? As the questions quickly reveal, one of the ways that environmental injustice perpetuates itself is by remaining invisible to those who benefit from the targeting of others. Only if you live next to the landfill, spend hours arguing with a slumlord about roaches, see the uranium waste trucked onto your reservation, happen to notice the defunct factories being crated for export, or stray off the beaten path and spot migrant workers' shacks do most people even think about who pays the price for the environmental hazards that make possible the high standard of living, health, and longevity commandeered by a fraction of the world's people.

THE IMPORTANT SCHOLAR and activist Robert D. Bullard explains that environmental racism is the foundational issue that environmental justice activists and scholars must attack. As he notes, worldwide, and especially in the United States and Europe, dominant-culture institutions are "providing advantages and privileges to whites while perpetrating segregation, underdevelopment, disenfranchisement, and the poisoning (some people would use the term genocide)" of people of color (8). Since its inception in the early 1990s, environmental justice as a concept and a movement has evolved, as even critics such as Ted Nordhaus and Michael Shellenberger acknowledge and as the special 2009 issue of *MELUS: Multi-Ethnic Literature of the United States* titled *Ethnicity and Ecocriticism* illustrates. In addition to issues of toxins and pollutants, which remain a priority, it encompasses concerns about transportation, education, unemployment, access to healthy food and health care, and global movements for food sovereignty, the struggle of small farmers around the world against corporate takeover. All interrelate in addressing problems confronted by poor people in economically depressed, negatively impacted environments that frequently have neither the economic nor the political power to win the NIMBY (Not In My Back Yard) argument. In particular, indigenous communities around the world face hugely disproportionate and often catastrophic environmental threats to members' health, lives, economic survival, and cultural and religious well-being because of multinational corporate and governmental policies and practices aimed at them.

In her 2002 essay "A Society Based on Conquest Cannot Be Sustained: Native Peoples and the Environmental Crisis," Anishinaabe scholar and activist Winona LaDuke lists well-known facts about this targeting:

> Over one million indigenous people will be relocated to allow for the development of hydroelectric dam projects in the next decade;
> The United States has detonated all its nuclear weapons in the lands of indigenous people, over six hundred of those tests within property belonging to the Shoshone nation;

Two-thirds of all uranium resources within the borders of the
    United States lie under Native reservations — in 1975, Indians
    produced 100 percent of all federally controlled uranium;
One-third of all low-sulphur coal in the western United States is on
    Indian land, with four of the ten largest coal strip mines in these
    same areas;
Fifteen of the current eighteen recipients of nuclear-waste research
    grants, so-called monitored retrievable nuclear storage sites, are
    Indian communities. (99)

Joel Kovel also lists several issues, using the beginning of the present
century, the year 2000, as a benchmark. Among other things:

Species were vanishing at a rate that has not occurred in 65 million
    years.
Fish were being taken at twice the rate as in 1970.
Forty percent of agricultural soils had been degraded.
Half of the forests had disappeared.
7.3 billion tons of pollutants were released in the United States
    during 1999.
The gap between rich and poor nations, according to the United Na-
    tions, went from a factor of . . . 35:1 in 1950 . . . to 72:1 in 1990. . . .
By 2000 1.2 million women under the age of eighteen were entering
    the global sex trade each year.
100 million children were homeless and slept on the streets. (2–3)

Reform cannot address the size and depth of the problem. The
achievement of environmental justice requires social transformation.
Richard Hofrichter calls for "major restructuring of the entire social

order." He argues that basic change begins with "a challenge to absolute property rights and the logic of industrial capitalism's emphasis on growth without limit" (5). Kovel points to the "screamingly obvious fact that a society predicated on endless expansion must inevitably collapse its natural base" (xiv). He states: "If we take this crisis seriously enough — and what, in the whole history of the human race, has had more momentous and dire implications? — then we are obliged to radically rethink our entire approach" (3). Kovel's vision of ecosocialism, to which I return in the next chapter and which corresponds in many ways with the views of Vine Deloria, Vandana Shiva, Simon Ortiz, Helena María Viramontes, Marilynne Robinson, Wendell Berry, and Gloria Naylor that I bring up in this one, holds out tremendous hope that people can come together to reorganize ourselves to live sustainably and justly. Kovel believes it is possible to live in ways that allow all human and other beings to survive on the planet Earth.

That will only happen, however, if there is spiritual revolution. Radical social transformation cannot come, indigenous thinkers in particular emphasize over and over again, until the so-called developed world undergoes a fundamental spiritual reorientation to an inclusively relational ethic that recognizes the place and value of all people, their communities, and the natural environment. This is the urgent work of the humanities in the twenty-first century. Yet David W. Orr points out, "We continue to educate the young for the most part as if there were no planetary emergency" (2), no need to make radical changes in thought and behavior. Environmental justice marks the place where the ecological crisis and the multicultural imperative meet, the place where a future committed to life, not death, can be built. Progressive people are the ones who can and must carry that message, which is not one of science or technology but of human values. What principles and beliefs will we — must we — embrace and abide by to reorder society so that people and all other life on the planet can survive?

WRITING IN 2008 from the prison cell where he has been unjustly held for more than three decades by the U.S. government, Lakota freedom fighter and activist Leonard Peltier reflects on the crisis now finally dawning on many Americans. "Our people have told them from the very beginning about the consequences of mistreatment of individuals and mistreatment of Mother Earth. There are history books that quote our chief headmen and medicine people cautioning them about their destruction of the earth and nature." The mindset that permits desecration of the earth is the same one that foments genocide, Peltier explains. "We know the first concentration camps America ever had held Indian prisoners. The first biological warfare was used on our people with poisonous blankets. The first atomic bomb was dropped on Indian land in Nevada. Today there are abandoned uranium quarries in Navajo country that cause genetic defects on a lot of their people." Environmental justice finally must come from the soul as well as the mind. It depends on making the connection named here by Peltier, seeing the linkage between violation of the earth, our mother, and exploitation and destruction of human and other beings, our sisters and brothers. Life on the planet is the issue at hand. Surely, no other question can be more pressing for humanists than this at this point in time.

# The People Who Pay

Native American and indigenous cultures worldwide have understood and experienced life as a continuum between human and nonhuman species and between present, past, and future generations. . . . Corporate globalization sees the world only as something to be owned and the market as only driven by profits. —Vandana Shiva, *Earth Democracy*

Acoma Pueblo poet and activist Simon Ortiz opens his 1999 volume of short stories *Men on the Moon* with a Pueblo grandfather in 1969 watching a wrestling match on TV. One fighter is Apache, the other white. The Apache wins, and immediately a new image appears: the Apollo spaceship on its launchpad about to head to the moon.

These two television images — a wrestling match between an Indian and a white man followed by the live broadcast of the Apollo moonshot — set up environmental justice themes in the book. Indian and white values lock in combat, as we see in the two wrestlers. And the white world has finally gone completely insane, as evidenced by the race to conquer space — the phallic flight to the moon where, upon arrival, three bizarrely dressed white men wearing machines on their bodies skip like boys and then float oddly as if underwater. The old man asks his grandson what they are doing. Are they looking for something? Knowledge, he is told, the origins of the universe. The grandfather is confused. "Well then, do they say why they need to know where and how everything began? Hasn't anyone ever told them?" (12). People have tried, his grandson replies, but the white people still don't know.

Placed first in the book, "Men on the Moon" enumerates basic Native American environmental justice issues: the military-industrial complex's drive for mastery of the universe, white people's refusal to listen to the wisdom of Native people, the elevation of Western science to the status of a god, the strange idea that some parts of the creation are not alive, and the West's rapacious consumption of natural resources. In the course of the story the grandfather has a vision of the destruction that this is producing, and the fiction ends with his hope that more wrestling will come on TV. He plans to root for the Apache.

Various Ortiz stories take up the literal environmental justice issue of exploitative labor practices. "Woman Singing" chronicles realities faced by Indian migrant workers in the potato fields of Idaho: the wretched housing, the constant dislocation and loneliness, the sexual exploitation of a woman worker by her employer. Worst is the killing escape of alcohol addiction encouraged by an economic system that has already stolen indigenous homelands and now attacks the workers' bodies and souls. The white potato-farm owner hands out biweekly wages and warns the workers to stay sober. Then he offers them a lift to the bar in town. In a similar vein "Crossing" remembers conditions early in the twentieth century when Pueblo men, their best farmland taken by invading whites, had no choice but to become migrants. The men are forced to accept jobs constructing and repairing railroad beds. The hopeless move plunges them into itinerancy, homelessness, poverty, violence, and alcohol.

These stories illustrate what is known as environmental job blackmail. You can accept the health-endangering job offered and live in poverty, get sick, and sooner or later die because of the employment. Or you and your family can starve. It makes no difference to predatory capitalism. There are more workers where you came from.

THE CONTEMPORARY CLASSIC by Helena María Viramontes, *Under the Feet of Jesus,* looks at this issue of environmental job blackmail in

California today. Dedicated to the memory of the great union activist César Chávez, the novel examines the entrapment of poor families, almost all of them Mexican or Mexican American, in lives of extreme poverty, homelessness, toxic poisoning, and government harassment so that other Americans — people with homes, health care, schools, and protected civil rights — can have obscenely cheap food. Central in Viramontes's novel, which Christa Grewe-Volpp quite rightly considers social realism, is Petra, a pregnant woman in her thirties who looks fifty. She and her family move with the crops from one cluster of migrant workers' shacks to another, all of them broken down, pest infested, and carefully placed far from any road or town where they might be seen by the people who eat the lettuce and grapes the migrants harvest. The five children and two adults sleep in one room, with Petra cooking and washing clothes over a fire in the dirt outside. No toilet or running water exists, and fertilizers and pesticides contaminate the water that is available. All go to the fields each day, the children working alongside the adults as soon as they are able.

Viramontes's novel is accurate. In the United States three years after *Under the Feet of Jesus* came out in 1995, the average annual income for a two-earner farmworker family was slightly more than $14,000, according to the National Center for Farmworker Health. The United States General Accounting Office in 2000 estimated that there were 300,000 fifteen- to seventeen-year-olds working in the fields, with no numbers for those younger. The United Farm Workers Union placed the overall number of child farmworkers at 800,000. Laws designed to protect these children have not been rewritten since 1938, which means that in most states a child under twelve may work unlimited hours with parental consent; at age sixteen the child may start doing hazardous things. Legislation mandating the amount of time that must elapse before workers reenter fields sprayed with pesticides is based on a 154-pound man. No exception is made for children, pregnant women, elders, or people already sick.

At a demonstration protesting anti-immigrant raids that I attended in October 2008, a physician explained the fear of deportation that keeps workers from seeking change or help. Because government officials invade medical clinics and emergency rooms, farmworkers where he treated people in California felt they had no choice but to drive up to the hospital door and drop unconscious, pesticide-poisoned fellow laborers on the sidewalk and then frantically drive away.

Petra abhors the degradation forced upon her and her children. *Under the Feet of Jesus* makes very clear that people do not choose to live in hovels or to fear constantly for the safety and health of their children, born and yet to be born. Petra worries that the baby growing within her will have deformities. She knows the excruciating fieldwork under a blazing sun in dirt filled with toxins from fertilizers and pesticides places her children's health in jeopardy. She can see how rapidly it is destroying the body of her unborn baby's father, Perfecto, a man much older and visibly deteriorating. The painful, bulging varicose veins in her own legs remind her that she too is breaking down because of the poverty, killing physical labor, anxiety, and homelessness.

*Under the Feet of Jesus* attacks many aspects of environmental injustice in the United States but above all the myth of meritocracy and the fact of internal colonialism. No group of people could work harder, longer, or for less than migrant laborers. Yet that work does *not* result in advancement, security, or prosperity. The belief that merit gets rewarded is a lie. Racism and an exploitative economic system collude to keep Petra and her family submerged in poverty, no matter how hard they work.

A vivid flashback early in the novel shows the literal hunger that forced Petra and her children from their tiny Los Angeles apartment into the migrant labor fields. When her oldest daughter, Estrella, looking in the cupboard for food, finds only dead roaches and an empty Quaker Oats box, the child angrily shakes the round, red-white-and-blue container. Her siblings begin to cry,

> and for a moment Estrella's eyes narrowed until Petra saw her headlock the Quaker man's paperboard head like a hollow drum and the twins sniffed their runny noses. One foot up, one foot down, her dress twirling like water loose in a drain, Estrella drummed the top of his low crown hat, slapped the round puffy man's double chins, beat his wavy long hair the silky color of creamy hot oats. . . . Estrella danced like a loca around the room around the bulging bags around Petra and in and out of the kitchenette and up and down the boxspring, her loud hammering tom-tom beats the only noise in the room. (19)

Physically pummeling the empty red-white-and-blue promise of full bellies and rosy cheeks that America — land of plenty — claims to provide, Estrella beats out her rage on the head of the smug, fat white man on the cardboard cylinder.

That man, of course, immediately evokes Benjamin Franklin. Indeed, his famous words in *Poor Richard's Almanac*, "Early to bed, early to rise, makes a man healthy, wealthy, and wise!" implicitly beckon from every Quaker Oats box. Work hard, and you will be rewarded. Franklin himself, so the well-known story goes, arrived in Philadelphia a barefoot boy with nothing. But he worked hard. He saved his pennies. He ended up rich, powerful, and enormously successful.

OK, *Under the Feet of Jesus* says. Petra and her family have nothing.

They work hard. They certainly collapse early at night and get up at the crack of dawn to head to the fields. So where is their health and wealth? To whom does the myth of meritocracy apply in the United States, and to whom is it a mockery, a hollow joke to make people loco? How does environmental racism target specific groups for disproportionate poverty and health hazards while allowing the majority of white people, like the foolish grinning patriarch on the Quaker Oats box, to believe that all is rosy?

The Quaker Oats scene ends with Petra recalling the back-breaking day labor that left her father's body wrecked and twisted. Then she thinks about Estrella trying to feed her hungry sisters and brothers with angry drumbeats and crazy dancing. Then she gets furious. She marches back to the apartment and children she fled in despair, crossing blaring lanes of L.A. traffic and making herself move: "One foot up, one foot down no more dancing with the full of empty Quaker man" (20). Now "Oats" is gone. It's simply the "full of empty Quaker man." That acid phrase says that even the best that white America has to offer — Quakers, famous for their pacifism and standing up to injustices such as slavery — rings hollow. In Viramontes's novel that patriotic, supposedly highly moral tradition does nothing but grin like a puffed-up idiot at the misery of the poor Chicano children who will pick the grapes that will become the raisins that will speckle the breakfast oats of fat white America.

Internal colonialism constantly shows its face in Petra's terror of La Migra, agents of the INS, or Immigration and Naturalization Service, renamed ICE, Immigration and Customs Enforcement, by the administration of George W. Bush. The new acronym proudly conveys the naked aggression Petra fears — to ice someone is slang for kill. Also, and not incidentally, ICE evokes the color white, along with freezing temperatures. Petra tells her children not to be intimidated. They are citizens. Their birth certificates lie carefully folded under the feet of Jesus, kept safe beneath the small statue of Jesucristo she carries from shack to shack. If accosted, the children must look at the agents squarely and refuse to be made to feel the United States is not their home.

How successful they will be is another question. As Robert Bullard points out, internal colonialism targeting Latinos, blacks, and indigenous people to benefit whites, especially economically, forms the very basis of the United States: "The nation was founded on the principles of 'free land' (stolen from Native Americans and Mexicans), 'free labor' (cruelly extracted from African slaves), and 'free men' (white men with property). From the outset, institutional racism shaped the economic, political, and ecological landscape, and buttressed the exploitation of both land and people" (16). When Petra says to her children, "Tell them que tienes una madre aquí. You are not an orphan, and she pointed a red finger to the earth, Aquí" (63), she is telling them to fight back. She insists on the truth that their ancestors, indigenous and Spanish, lived on the land long before white northern Europeans ever laid eyes on what is now California.

But even if Petra's family did not have legal documentation, as many of their fellow migrant workers do not, her words "una madre aquí" make this point: by what right does a nation that stole its land from Native people and Mexico and now steals the labor and health of workers forced by economics to cross arbitrary borders to harvest crops that feed the rich claim that those workers do not belong? As immigrant rights activists repeatedly point out, undocumented workers almost always come to the United States for two related reasons. Their economies have been devastated more often than not by global economic policies and practices invented in and supported by the United States, and employers in the United States are all too happy to hire people unable to demand rights out of fear of deportation. Petra's words "una madre aquí" call into the text the truth Vandana Shiva names in *Earth Democracy*: "Most sustainable cultures, in all their diversity, view the earth as *terra mater* (mother earth)" (22). Also they stress the fact, emphasized by Shiva, that the construct of colonialism dismisses that truth. It reserves space and rights for an elite while cutting the poor off, labeling their presence illegal, illegitimate. But the words "una madre aquí" render the concept of orphan itself fraudulent, as Petra's act of taking into her own family a dying migrant child laborer without parents, Alejo, shows. Una madre the earth has no orphans. Much less illegals.

THE HISTORIC First National People of Color Environmental Leadership Summit in Washington, D.C., in 1991 issued seventeen Principles of Environmental Justice. The first states: "*Environmental justice* affirms the sacredness of Mother Earth, ecological unity and the interdependence of all species, and the right to be free from ecological destruction." The following sixteen articulate ecological and social justice truths agreed upon by the leaders. They include the equal right of all to protection from nuclear, toxic, and other environmental hazards; the equal right of all to clean air, water, land, and food; the equal right of all to political and cultural self-determination and decision making; the equal right of all to freedom from environmental job blackmail, with accountability for those who perpetrate it; and the equal responsibility of all to live in ways that contribute to the health of the planet. Underlying each of these principles is rejection of market-driven greed and disrespect for life.

That greed and disrespect — for people, for the earth — feed the cultural imperialism that Simon Ortiz indicts in *Men on the Moon* in

"What Indians Do," a series of vignettes that reveal some of the countless ways in which economic exploitation of the earth and racist exploitation of Native people interconnect and permeate Indians' lives all the time. The narrative begins with a conversation about space exploration that echoes the volume's opening. An old uncle, pointing to his own breast, says of Western scientists: "But they don't know that they should look into the space that is in here" (129). It goes on to quote a *San Francisco Examiner* headline that proudly shouts: "PRIVATE PROPERTY WEEK BEGINS TODAY." Promised "the truth about Uncle Sam," the narrator imagines the article will be about environmental injustice. "I thought the *Examiner* would tell about U.S. corporations building suburbs outside Albuquerque and Phoenix on Indian lands, taking what little water Indians have left. I thought it would tell about the Indians pocketed into tiny leftover enclaves in San Diego County. But, of course, it didn't" (132). Another vignette shows U.S. Forest Service archaeologists refusing to talk about the real issues impacting indigenous people — superhighways, multi-million-dollar mining operations, water and land theft. And at a session titled "The Anthropologist and the Indian" at an academic conference, we see the white experts hold forth so long about preserving Indians that the narrator never even gets to hear the invited living indigenous speaker.

Cutting back and forth between colonial theft of land and resources and racist theft of indigenous identity and voice, "What Indians Do" presents the bitter reality of cultural imperialism for Native people. As Laurie Anne Whitt explains, cultural imperialism makes use of myriad forms of acquisition — legal, material, intellectual — to appropriate and profit from Indian lands, beliefs, and identities. In "What Indians Do" dominant-culture mastery of the earth through private property and resource confiscation and racist mastery of Native peoples through silencing and erasure emerge as completely interdependent phenomena. Each requires the other for its successful accomplishment, and both come from exactly the same basic Western ethic of insatiable conquest and dominance.

The deep pathology of that ethic appears in many places in Ortiz's volume but nowhere more horribly than in the story "Distance." On a nice white family farm a spirited young billy goat, George, butts and knocks down the farmer's little girl. Her knee is scraped, so she cries. The farmer says kindly, "We'll get that old goat tamed down" (163). He then proceeds to torture the animal to death by withholding water. As the days pass, the goat strains against the rope holding him, his legs weaken, he falls to his knees, his bleats stop, his eyes glaze. The little girl asks when he can be loose again. "The father looked at his little girl, and he smiled and said, 'When George learns, sweetheart, when George learns not to be so mean'" (165). Slowly dehydrated by the calm, superior white father protecting his darling in an exercise of brute force that he defines as "taming," the goat is murdered for being a goat, for being a created being with his own spirit and will. For readers, George is a living being sadistically subjugated until he dies. For the white farmer, George is property to be dealt with as he wishes.

"Distance" forces us to confront the spiritual sickness at the heart of the dominant ethic of conquest, exploitation, and ownership that the environmental justice movement mobilizes against. In "A Society Based on Conquest Cannot Be Sustained" LaDuke explains that "the system of capitalism and other forms of industrialism . . . lack respect for people and their environments in an insatiable quest for resources. This is particularly obvious in the United States, which consumes one-third of the world's resources and hosts only 5 percent of the world's population." LaDuke directly ties such wholesale and wanton abuse of

the earth to the ethic of conquest motivating Columbus and respon-
sible for genocide in the Americas: "Columbus provided the entrée for
this system into the Western hemisphere. The holocaust that subse-
quently occurred in the Americas is unparalleled on a world scale, and
in its wake was the disruption necessary to destroy many indigenous
economic and governmental systems. It is the most comprehensive system of imperialism ever witnessed by humanity. While no one knows
exactly how many people were killed since Columbus's invasion, one
conservative estimate suggests that the population of indigenous people in 1492 was 112,554,000 in the Western hemisphere and 28,264,000
in 1980" (101).

My students often ask, How could Europeans and European Americans do what they have done to indigenous people in the Americas? How
could people systematically murder thousands — millions — of other
people? "Distance," I believe, answers with this question: how does
the farmer murder George? The story speaks to the history of Western
colonial violence against Native peoples. Massacring unarmed people
and abusing children in the many Indian boarding schools mentioned
by Ortiz, controlling and withholding the earth's water and other resources, calling the land empty in order to steal it, forcing all created
beings such as George to submit to white authority and ideology or
die — all are of one piece. The same value scheme dictates all four.

Ortiz's story is not an allegory. Although it has powerful allegorical
resonances, it is literally and importantly about a white man denying
another living being the sacred right to his own life. Vine Deloria, Jr.,
states in the original 1973 edition of *God Is Red*: "Any violation of another entity's right to existence in and of itself is a violation of the nature of the creation and a degradation of religious reality itself" (299).
The deadly dominant ethic that the farmer embraces cannot conceive

of people as simply one part of the creation. The farmer's philosophy insists on human beings as supreme, the rulers of the earth, the apex of creation, and then himself as the apex of the apex. If we read the story as an allegory, we erase that literal, lethal arrogance and reduce George to a symbol, denying his equal right to his own life and identity in the creation. We ironically reproduce, in other words, precisely the Western blindness that the text makes horrifying.

As "Distance" suggests, the problem that environmental justice addresses is at bottom spiritual: the alienation of modern culture from the earth, the learned ignorance with reference to the sacred nature of life in all its forms: lunar, goat, human, interstellar. Huge relearning must take place for justice and healing to occur.

## Mind Shifts

Within the traditions, beliefs, and customs of the American Indian people are the guidelines for society's future. — Vine Deloria, Jr., *God Is Red*

Marilynne Robinson's best-selling late-twentieth-century novel, *Housekeeping*, traces the soul-deadening toll on white people of Western ideologies of endless progress and resource consumption. In the tradition of Pauline Hopkins's rewrite of *The Tempest*, Robinson revises the story of Noah and the flood — *Housekeeping* is full of rising waters and the question of who will survive and who will not. It further invokes the Old Testament with the main character's name, Ruth. But also, the opening line, "My name is Ruth," deliberately calls up the opening line, "Call me Ishmael," of the nineteenth-century white American classic *Moby-Dick*. It brings to mind a book literally about conquering, killing, and chopping up animals for fuel — whale oil — to burn in civilization's lamps. And *Moby-Dick*, of course, is about whiteness as something to be feared: that is, both Ahab and the whale.

*Housekeeping* yearns for a world outside the European American ethos of battling nature. It resists the Western mindset of constantly trying to shape and control the created world to assert and enforce human superiority. While still a child, Ruth gravitates to her rebellious, itinerant aunt Sylvia (Latin for "woods"), who refuses the patriarchal injunction of Genesis to subdue and master the earth. Sylvia's housekeeping allows leaves, water, and insects to blow, flow, and fly through the house, just as they do through the woods and fields outside. Adult and child eat in the dark, burning no lights. Ruth goes to school or doesn't. Earth's seasons and rhythms, not the rules of the town patriarchs, guide their lives — to the horror and eventual censure of civic leaders. So Sylvia and Ruth simply leave. They become transients.

Robinson's novel is open to the charge of romanticizing homelessness and poverty. Who but a privileged white person caught in the clutch of late-twentieth-century angst and alienation could possibly imagine dirt-poor life on the run — sleeping in boxcars, begging for scraps at the backdoor of a restaurant — as preferable to four walls and a roof and food on the table? But that misses the point of the book, which is not literal. *Housekeeping* and *Walden* are not saying everyone should hit the road or live in a hut in the woods. Rather, Robinson's novel, like *Winona*, offers a serious fantasy, a parable. Its activism consists of its saying no *as a white-authored text* to the dominant-culture norms of conformity, industriousness, and acquisition on which the United States prides itself. *Housekeeping* examines the myth of meritocracy from the opposite side of *Under the Feet of Jesus*. Being white, native born, and literate, Sylvia probably could work hard and make money. She probably could join Ben Franklin. So could Ruth. But for what? Robinson asks. Almost all the obedient whites in Fingerbone, the emaciated name of the town in this novel, seem numb and caged, like Ruth's sister at the end who thrives materially but hungers spiritually. Or they literally kill themselves.

*Housekeeping* says that Judeo-Christian values must return to respect for nature in order for the suicide course of the contemporary world to stop. When Ruth and Sylvia — and we with them — walk away from built Western structures of confinement and mastery, they choose to live in harmony with the earth's truth that excess accumulation and attempts to conquer nature are insane. Their election of transience reminds us that we are all transients. The book is not about literal social science solutions to the postmodern hollowness and soul-sickness that centuries of white patriarchal dominance have produced. It is about the need for radical spiritual revolution as the necessary first step in any significant change of course. Ruth must follow Sylvia. Judeo-Christian values must return to an understanding that we are part of, not masters of, the earth.

THAT RADICAL SPIRITUAL revolution, in the opinion of white environmental justice writer Wendell Berry and black liberation theologian James Cone as well as many others, involves regrounding Judeo-Christianity in respect for the earth. When Berry reflects on the crime and sin of strip mining in Kentucky in *A Continuous Harmony*, he opens with a line from Jeremiah, the same Old Testament prophet who inspired the justice rhetoric of David Walker. Berry chooses this epigraph: "... *they have made my pleasant field a desolate wilderness* ... —JEREMIAH 12:10." Then he explains that there are two ways to regard the earth:

So far as I know, there are only two philosophies of land use. One holds that the earth is the Lord's, or it holds that the earth belongs to those yet to be born as well as to those now living. The present owners, according to this view, only have the land in trust, both for all the living who are dependent on it now, and for the unborn who will be dependent on it in time to come. . . .

The other philosophy is that of exploitation, which holds that the interest of the present owner is the only interest to be considered. The standard, according to this view, is profit, and it is assumed that whatever is profitable is good. (169–70)

Cone reasons in *Risks of Faith* that the environmental movement needs to address racism, including within its own ranks. But he also emphasizes that liberation theology, which condemns racism, must broaden itself to understand that abuse of the planet and abuse of people interconnect.

*Housekeeping* and *Under the Feet of Jesus* agree with Berry's condemnation of profit as the highest good. Viramontes, in addition, shares Cone's belief that the Christianity of oppressed people of color can offer an alternative to global capitalism's creed of exploitation and desecration. In *Under the Feet of Jesus* the crucifixion of Christ, the hope signaled by his birth in a barn, and the earth-based sacred power of the Virgen de Guadalupe appear in subtle but unmistakable images. Each upholds liberation theology's insistence on Christianity as a faith of this-world activist demands for justice. Each defines the most despised — in this case, migrant workers — as Christ's brothers and sisters. The airplane that sprays Alejo with pesticides casts the shadow of the cross on the little boy as it spews its poisons. The barn full of swallows, sweet decaying hay, and soft silent darkness where the courageous child Estrella finds peace and strength is repeatedly called a cathedral, and the book ends with that dark-skinned girl bursting through the holy building's rotted roof into the evening sky full of glittering stars and fluttering birds. The image clearly evokes icons of the Virgen de Guadalupe, the holy mother who revealed herself first in the Americas to an indigenous person and who represents a champion of justice for many Mexicans and Mexican Americans of faith.

THE HINTS OF Robinson and Viramontes confirm the arguments of Berry, Cone, Cornel West, Michael Lerner, Katie Cannon, Jim Wallis, Karen Armstrong, and many others that Western religious values can guide the activist struggle for social and environmental justice. It is a difficult position for many people to accept. The overwhelming record of Christianity in particular is one of hatred, destruction, theft, and violence. The facts, past and present, are dismal. John Brown was a Christian, true. But so was Col. John Chivington, the Methodist minister who led the Third Colorado Regulars in the massacre of unarmed Cheyenne and Arapaho women, men, and children at Sand Creek in 1864 and then headed the military parade through the streets of Denver, where U.S. soldiers displayed the murder victims' genitals on their hats and saddles. The atrocities gleefully boasted of by U.S. soldiers at Abu Ghraib Prison early in the twenty-first century, including the holy war that landed them in Iraq in the first place, have a long history in the United States. That history is drenched in Christian hatred and national commitment to destructive paradigms of dominance and subordination, superiority and inferiority, chosen and damned.

Christianity contains within it, like the other Abrahamic religions, Judaism and Islam, a lethal value-set alongside the liberatory one invoked by liberation theology and liberal activists of faith. More than forty years ago environmental historian Lynn White, Jr., indicted Christianity, along with post-Christianity in his view, for teaching us to believe that "we are *not* . . . part of the natural process. We are superior to nature, contemptuous of it, willing to use it for our slightest whim" (12). As Robert Warrior makes crystal clear, the very concept of a chosen people and a promised land requires oppression. Biblical Jews invaded Canaan, and today Israelis claim a divine right to place Palestinians under house arrest in their own land. European and American Christians murdered and stole land from indigenous people in the Americas for centuries, and that process continues today by means of institutionalized poverty and environmental devastation. The legacy of Judeo-Christian belief — as, indeed, William Apess, David Walker, Harriet Beecher Stowe, Cornel West, Jim Wallis, Michael Lerner, Wendell Berry, Katie Cannon, and James Cone fully recognize — has been one of terrible abuse of both people and the earth.

A number of years ago in Cincinnati, Ohio, I accepted an invitation on a miserable winter night to visit the storefront evangelical Christian church where people I knew, along with other urban migrants from Appalachia, all of them very poor, worshiped. In the steamy room the service ended with the charismatic, ecstatic, white-suited preacher, Brother Dave, an extremely sexy, blue-eyed version of Elvis Presley, climbing up on a huge neon-lit cross. There he arched his back tragically and flung his arms out to each side, Christ-like. Then the collection was taken up, and I watched people who I knew did not have money for milk for their children empty every cent they had into the basket.

Faith — belief — is not in and of itself a liberatory thing, or a good one. It can easily revictimize the already victimized, as Brother Dave's bulging wallet and the missionary depredations of Christian colonialism worldwide, the violence of fundamentalist Zionism, and the misogyny of right-wing Islam only underscore today. Christianity especially has been put to hideous use, justifying slavery and genocide in the Americas and defending the predatory capitalism that devastates the planet and destroys the lives of millions of poor people around the world in our own time. Some courageous, visionary activists of faith such as Cone, Wallis, West, Lerner, and Cannon believe that Judeo and Judeo-Christian values can be reclaimed to serve social justice and planetary health, and their words and actions inspire many in the struggle for progressive social change.

Others, however, believe that the spiritual values we need can never come from Abrahamic religions.

## Earth Knowledge

We have a problem of two separate spiritual paradigms and one dominant culture — make that a dominant culture with an immense appetite for natural resources. — Winona LaDuke, *Recovering the Sacred*

Gloria Naylor's *Mama Day* says that traditional West African spiritual beliefs and practices traveled with enslaved people to North America and that those ways of knowing the sacred, ways far older than and much different from Christianity, offer radical possibilities for healing in the postmodern world. The novel dramatizes historians' findings, which many black Americans like Naylor had already known. Despite the terrible Middle Passage and centuries of enslavement and then discrimination, African-derived cultural practices and earth-based religious beliefs survive in North America. They continue to have power, particularly among African Americans in the southern United States who live on and work the land.

Naylor also shows in *Mama Day*, as Patricia Klindienst records in *The Earth Knows My Name*, that the memory of slavery lives in the land itself. The soil still knows the blood and toil of ancestors, and that knowledge is fact, not metaphor. As Ralph Middleton, an elder in the Gullah community on St. Helena Island off the coast of South Carolina, explains in *The Earth Knows My Name*, "After slavery, most blacks stayed on the land here. We feel that we are part of the land. . . . This is where we've been, where we've worked, for generations. You know your grandparents and great-grandparents planted here. We have memories about the land, about what they did here. So it's important. It's sacred" (37). Klindienst and Naylor write in the activist hope that all people will relearn the sacred from the land, the elders who honor it, and the ancestors whose spirits abide.

AS A LITERAL environmental justice text, *Mama Day* attacks the issue of development — the rapacious consumption of small black-owned farms and entire Gullah communities to build golf courses, condominiums, vacation homes, and gated enclaves for rich white people. Naylor's central character, Mama Day, won't sell. She will not allow land farmed renewably for generations and reverenced for the human souls it sustained and the blood of slaves it absorbed to become merely property — a dead thing. The novel illustrates activists' point that development on the Sea Islands and all along the southern U.S. Atlantic coast does more than displace poor people. It destroys entire cultures and belief systems. It means that the earth is no longer valued for the nourishment, medicine, and spiritual knowledge it provides. Land becomes simply a commodity prized for the surplus wealth and conspicuous leisure its acquisition symbolizes — plus, of course, the exclusion, all those fences, it enforces.

That exclusion, as Ruth Perry explains in an important ecofeminist argument in the activist tradition of Annette Kolodny or Cheryll Glotfelty, has its origins in the industrial revolution and the commercialization of agriculture in eighteenth- and early-nineteenth-century England. Land enclosure created a middle-class gender split that continues to define economic thought and practice today. Men's work in the world, whether done by men or women, counts in the GNP (gross national product). That means it exists in the monetary economy and therefore has value. But the traditional unpaid reproductive labor of women, the work of raising children, keeping house, cooking meals, caring for the elderly, tending family emotions, running errands — all the maintenance work still done mostly by women and without which the paid economy would grind to a halt — shows up nowhere in the GNP. Without this unpaid reproductive labor, the paid economy could not function. But it is rendered invisible and therefore worthless by conventional economics, which know only one way to measure value: money, bank accounts, real estate, the GNP.

Perry uses the example of wetlands to show how this thinking legitimizes ecologically devastating development such as that in Naylor's book. A wetland does crucial work for the planet and all life on it by fixing nitrogen and recycling carbon, cleansing water and air of toxins, and nurturing plant and animal life necessary to the natural balance. In other words, a wetland is not simply nice to have around. It is indispensable to the health and survival of plant and animal life, ourselves included. But it contributes nothing to the GNP. It constitutes unpaid reproductive labor and therefore has no value, according to mainstream economic measures. Consequently, its protection gets easily overridden by developers' monetary arguments, and millions of acres of so-called empty land — which is really densely inhabited and highly productive — turn into big-box stores, shopping malls, and fancy second homes.

Environmental justice takes a stand against the way this destructive thinking targets not just the earth and its nonhuman life forms but also the people on earth labeled not-there, economically unimportant. In the background of *Mama Day* developers constantly nip at the African American sea-island community, threatening their sustainable way of life by dangling huge sums of money for land and enticing their children to leave. The book shows the living history, the communal earth-based way of life, and the deeply spiritual Africa-derived *healing* values — values that the postmodern Western world desperately needs — that Mama Day fiercely defends in the face of development and all of us should protect and embrace as well.

*Mama Day*, with its insistence on the need for radical moral reorientation, offers a rewrite of *The Tempest* even more audacious than Hopkins's. In Gloria Naylor's novel not only is Prospero reimagined, he is replaced. The elder with incredible powers that Western thought labels magic but indigenous thought worldwide understands as earth based is not an old white man but an old black woman: Mama Day. Like Prospero, she presides over a stormy tropical island in the Atlantic Ocean off the coast of North America, and her birth name, Miranda, leaves no doubt that Naylor wants us to recall Shakespeare's famous fantasy about the origins of slavery and empire in the so-called New World. Naylor's Miranda, however, rejects the market mentality of the white slaveholding father. She lives instead by the values of the black mother: the ancestor who suffered slavery's horror, survived, and triumphed, retaining truths from Africa through the dark Middle Passage and the long years of captivity and then learning new ones from the earth in North America.

Mama Day knows which plants cure which illnesses. She knows the rituals that relieve human infertility. She knows how to hear the dead, who do speak. She knows the earth's energy can be used for evil as well as good. She knows conjure is real, and human hands contain the power to heal.

None of this is symbolic. It is literally, materially true in *Mama Day*. George, a young black engineer from the other important island in the book, Manhattan, responds to Mama Day's medicinal instructions with confusion. From his urban secular point of view she speaks in metaphors. But as Mama Day reflects: "Metaphors. Like what they used in poetry and stuff. The stuff folks dreamed up when they was making a fantasy, while what she was talking about was *real*. As real as them young hands in front of her" (294). The truth that Mama Day needs George to comprehend is spoken of by Ralph Middleton in more conventional terms in *The Earth Knows My Name* when he states: "The land is God." Then he adds: "And the land is God's. We see God walking through it. We're just caretakers" (63). In *Mama Day* Naylor urges us to see that African American spiritual and material wisdom rooted in non-Western African beliefs as well as in the soil of the American South where the blood of slaves fell can bring healing and new life. It is possible for George (Washington?) to learn to think and act outside the boxed universe of contemporary Manhattan. It is possible for people from the sea island's paved-over, postmodern antithesis — the place where most readers, figuratively, if not literally, sit reading the novel — to change, to understand the world differently.

IN MY 2007 CLASS on environmental justice and U.S. literature, one of the students explained that he hoped to become a surgeon. He told his classmates he believed it was a sacred calling. "When you hold a person's heart in your hands," he said, "you hold their soul." Most class members looked confused. Others were embarrassed at the naked emotional admission. I thought to myself that *Mama Day* had started to join us.

## Old Light

It is by the affirmation of knowledge of source and place and spiritual return that resistance is realized.
— Simon Ortiz, "Towards a National Indian Literature"

In Simon Ortiz's *Men on the Moon* uranium mines reveal the gargantuan lust of the energy conglomerate Kerr-McGee. Also and less expected, they create a context where change can occur, where spiritual transformation might begin if non-Indians are willing to listen to indigenous people.

Now a subsidiary of Anadarko Petroleum, Kerr-McGee in the 1960s and 1970s, the time frame of Ortiz's mining stories, operated the huge Ambrosia Lake uranium mine in New Mexico that provides the setting for his fictions. Most people probably know Kerr-McGee because of activist Karen Silkwood's successful environmental justice lawsuit in 1979, made into the 1983 movie *Silkwood*, which inspired *Erin Brockovich* in 2000. But the mining company also made the news in the 1970s for other environmental hazards harming people, animals, and the earth. It conducted an experiment to test the idea of using treated liquid uranium waste as fertilizer for grassland grazed by beef cattle. It also served as an industry model for the practice of backfilling active mines with uranium tailings to shore up collapsing walls around the workers with toxic waste by-products. Today, the site of the Ambrosia Lake mine contains the largest pile of uranium tailings in the Western world.

Ortiz's "To Change Life in a Good Way" tells of the friendship between two Kerr-McGee mining families, a Laguna Pueblo couple, Pete and Mary, and a white couple, Bill and Ida. The story moves back and forth between a mine as the dangerous place where the men work bringing up ore from the earth and a mine as the weapon that accidentally kills Bill's brother, Slick, in the Vietnam War. The two American mines — one just below the surface of the ground and openly designed to kill, the other deeply below ground and supposedly just a job but also deadly — get all confused in Bill's mind. He can't suppress the thought that his brother's own country killed him.

As Bill struggles to figure out what his brother died for — "Well, because of the mine, stepping on the wrong place, being in a dangerous place, but something else" (115) — his dawning awareness guides the reader's. The wrong place that the young white man stepped was Vietnam, Sand Creek, Wounded Knee, Abu Ghraib. The mine-made-in-America that blew him up is the imperialism poor people have been taught from the founding of the nation to fight for, as in the war in Iraq in the early twenty-first century, in order to make rich men richer. But also the mine-made-in-America that blew Slick up is Kerr-McGee itself, the violent, dangerous, ticking bomb in the earth that poisons miners, pollutes the soil, air, and water on which indigenous people in particular depend, and provides the raw materials to conduct the modern warfare that sends Slick halfway around the world to die.

Environmental justice scholar Joni Seager points out that the U.S. military creates enormous environmental devastation that national security arguments shield from regulation. As Winona LaDuke and many other indigenous activists emphasize, almost all of those devastating military operations are located on Indian land. That is the connection Ortiz's story literally makes. "To Change Life in a Good Way" links U.S. military imperialism — Slick's death — to the basic environmental justice issue of people of color and poor whites — Pete and Bill — being disproportionately impacted by the toxic practices of hugely profitable corporations that fuel war and force poor people to choose between health and a paycheck.

In addition, however, Ortiz's story voices the underlying environmental justice need for radical dominant-culture spiritual reorientation. When Pete and Mary hear of Slick's death, they make a Laguna prayer bundle for their white friends. They also give them an ear of Indian corn. Although Pete doesn't know all the old words or exact rituals, he does know the sacred bundle can help Slick on his journey and aid the living. He tells Bill: "It's just for Slick. For his travel from this life among us to another place of being. You and Ida and Slick are not Indian, but it doesn't make any difference. It's for all of us, this kind of way, with corn and with this, Bill. You take these sticks and feathers and you put them somewhere you think you should, someplace important that you think might be good, maybe to change life in a good way, that you think Slick would be helping us with" (113). Bill takes the bundle deep into the mine at Kerr-McGee, leaving it for Slick with words of newfound respect for Indian beliefs. His wife plans to plant the ear of Indian corn. Ortiz's story says that Laguna wisdom — given in friendship, not something that can be bought, taken, demanded — may ease Slick's journey and may stop Kerr-McGee from killing more miners. A new crop may be able to take root in white people's gardens.

Ortiz's story is not about non-Native people becoming wannabes: fake or imitation Indians. It is about non-Indians listening to and following the religious wisdom that indigenous people have not forgotten and others may also know if friendship and humility guide them. Nor does Ortiz's story present modern-day Noble Savages, New Age stereotypes of essentialized primitives somehow innately programmed to cherish the earth and reject all things Western. Pete and Mary are Laguna people who have survived five hundred years of colonial assault with enough of the old knowledge intact to understand the basic spiritual truth that all of creation is sacred and to be lived with in balance, not in a hierarchy of dominance and subordination, conquest and rape, profit and plunder. Awiakta explains in *Selu* that "Western thought is based on dichotomies, which separate spirit from matter, thought from feeling, and so on . . . and that detachment has increased in a society now geared to technology and the domination of nature" (241), a society, Ortiz maintains, that is tearing the earth apart for profit and can't wait to colonize the moon. But the sacred inheres in the material world. The two are not different realms, much less hierarchically arranged ones.

ECHOING "To Change Life," the white narrator in Ortiz's "Hiding, West of Here," son and grandson of West Virginia coal miners and now a mechanic at Kerr-McKee's Ambrosia Lake mine, takes us with him into the mountains on his day off. When two Native men come into view, the narrator, unseen, watches them take out a prayer bundle, sing, and then place the bundle in a crack in a large rock. He realizes they are praying and that he, because he is there, is part of the prayer, even though the men don't see him. Into his mind come the West Virginia strip mines and how the earth must have looked before the mining and still does look in places. He senses the thought means something, but what? The Native men leave. The story ends with the white man quiet and still feeling part of the prayer.

This story reiterates the truth that non-Natives must learn from Indians. The "Hiding" narrator does not need anyone to tell him to get out of the mine, the town, the house, the shopping center, the bar, the church and enter the mountains on a Sunday. He knows where he needs to be. What he does not know is how to pray there. Ortiz's nameless white (every?)man understands at some level that the earth is sacred, should not be strip-mined, should be honored and thanked. Deep in him are those truths. To find them, however, he must listen to those indigenous people who still remember the sacredness of creation, in this case Indians. And he must do so in a spirit of respect or hiding — not intruding, appropriating, presuming, leading, or otherwise reproducing the colonial arrogance that has brought the world to its present disastrous state. Then he may become part of a prayer that leads, as we see in the story's last line, to a vision: a human being in the quiet, in the mountains, in prayer, not alone.

A BASIC DIFFERENCE between Judeo-Christian and indigenous religions according to Vine Deloria, Jr., has to do with Native religions being place based and experiential. Deloria explains that instead of creeds, doctrines, sermons, and theological arguments driving and dictating belief, indigenous religions understand that knowledge of the sacred comes to humans experientially and that those experiences occur at certain places on the earth. Therefore, as he stresses in *God Is Red*, "unless the sacred places are discovered and protected and used as religious places, there is no possibility of a nation ever coming to grips with the land itself. Without this basic relationship, national psychic stability is impossible" (291). Environmental justice from indigenous points of view can never be simply about economics or politics or social equity. As *God Is Red, Selu, Recovering the Sacred,* and stories such as "To Change Life in a Good Way" and "Hiding, West of Here" explain, environmental justice must always be grounded, literally, in place-based and experientially arrived-at spiritual values.

In *Men on the Moon* Simon Ortiz takes tremendous risks. The history of European American theft of Indian land, lives, bones, children, health, resources, art, stories, and religion is so long and horrendous that the mere suggestion that white people might participate in Native spiritual ways, even at a distance, carries with it the danger of encouraging further colonial crimes. Indigenous scholars and activists and non-Natives allied in the struggle against anti-Indian racism uniformly condemn the racism and cultural imperialism of non-Natives pretending to be Indian, finding the hidden Indian within, discovering their long-lost Cherokee princess great-grandmother, deciding to write fake Indian books, setting up shop as "shamans," descending on reservations to acquire wisdom, or hiring out as supposedly indigenous healers.

Ortiz's fiction is *not* suggesting whites or any other non-Native people try to become Indians. "To Change Life in a Good Way" is saying that hope and healing have the possibility of coming from bonds between all people exploited by the system of late capitalism and indigenous people oppressed by Western economic practices for centuries, *if* the non-Natives are able to approach such affiliation in a spirit of respect and thus learn from indigenous people how to see and live life differently. "Hiding, West of Here" suggests, further, that the potential for that changed awareness already lives in at least some people who are not indigenous. A memory exists that can be awakened, a desire that wishes to express itself, as the repeated trips of the white man into the mountains and therefore into the prayer of the Pueblo men reveal.

Each story says that transformation — tentative, very fragile, but a beginning — is possible.

All living things now stand on the brink of oblivion and extinction.
—Vine Deloria, Jr., "Vision and Community"

The choice we make will decide whether or not we survive as a species.
—Vandana Shiva, *Soil Not Oil*

# FIVE

## Jesus, Marx, and the Future of the Planet

Women's studies conferences and panels in the United States have taught me many things about literature, history, societal norms, economic disparities, health issues, reproductive rights, sexuality struggles, political hurdles, and the fight to end racism. But not until I attended the International Women's Studies Conference in Kampala, Uganda, in 2002 had I seen a program with multiple sessions on water.

The Uganda conference, organized and attended almost entirely by African women, opened my eyes. A two-week-long economics seminar in Ghana a few years earlier had shown me how the World Bank and the International Monetary Fund operate, I believed. But I was wrong. Only when I listened to women in Uganda describe the privatization and sale of water in South African townships did the human reality emerge. Speakers explained how multinational corporations have been replacing communal spigots with coin-operated meters. For the women who gather to draw water for their family's needs and who have little or no money, this means that a life necessity has become unavailable or so very scarce as to be health endangering, all for the purpose of turning a profit halfway around the world in some rich cosmopolitan capital. There, corporate officers — aptly named, for it is a war — never see the dehydration, disease, infant mortality, and increasingly lethal poverty that their bright new idea of selling water produces. Indeed, the idea is such a clever one that, incredibly, multinational soft drink companies have successfully convinced privileged people in the North not to drink perfectly safe, free, publicly provided water. Instead, they now buy it in millions of plastic bottles, big and small, the production, transportation, and disposal of which consume incalculable amounts of nonrenewable fossil fuels and the political price of which is a whole generation of people not committed to safe water for all as a basic human right.

Globalization does connect us. It means poor people in the South are forced into buying water they cannot afford while rich people in the North are brainwashed into buying water they do not need. It means all of us are manipulated to fill the coffers of multinational corporations. The major difference is that the people in the South know this is insane — and wrong. Water, like the other gifts of the earth, should not be for sale.

# Looking South

This is the face of globalization, with capital racing across the planet and sucking nature and humanity into its maw.—Joel Kovel, *The Enemy of Nature*

Global capital uses debt as a weapon. When OPEC money flooded into Western banks in the middle of the twentieth century, banks used it to earn interest and therefore make a profit by issuing huge loans to developing nations under conditions laid down by the World Bank and the International Monetary Fund (IMF). Designed to advantage the rich lending countries in the North not only by providing interest but also, and much more important, by dictating trade, manufacturing, labor, and environmental policies that benefit the North and especially the United States, these "structural adjustment loans" constitute what many environmental justice scholars and activists such as Robert Weissman, Walden Bello, Vandana Shiva, and Joel Kovel, to name just a few, identify as a global economic war targeting the earth's majority, which is to say, poor people of color.

Between the end of World War Two and the conservative Reagan era of the 1980s, many nations in the Southern Hemisphere began to develop economic health and autonomy as they claimed independence from centuries of Western colonial dominance. The World Bank and IMF loans, however, quickly reversed that process. The huge debt they impose recolonizes developing nations because most cannot meet the interest payments. They therefore fall farther and farther behind even as the World Bank and IMF continue to exert socioeconomic control by means of disadvantageous policies. Those include, typically, mandates to lower tariffs on goods from the lending countries, which then inundate and skew local markets and production; requirements to increase certain exports and prohibit others, which distorts local economies and destroys economic diversity and therefore sustainability; and provisions to allow in multinational corporations without the kinds of controls on fair wages, workplace safety, child labor, and environmental standards required in the developed world. All of this depends on the creation of corrupt oligarchic elites and nondemocratic governments in these "client states" — states in which the poor just get poorer. The resulting socioeconomic reality coupled with the gargantuan interest payments that can never be met institutionalize a neocolonial cycle of debt, dependency, poverty, and environmental devastation in poor nations of the South.

What this means is clear. Globalization impoverishes the South and destroys its environment to enrich the North. It is environmental job blackmail writ globally, and the effects of this predatory economic assault on the planet, people, resources, and all living beings will not, as anyone paying attention now must see, stay contained in one part of the world. The consequences of empire always come home to roost.

There are signs of change.

More and more people in the North are beginning to question the morality of poisoning workers and the planet in one place so that protected people in another can go to big-box stores to fill shopping carts with mounds of cheap goods. Also, toxic colonialism — the practice of dumping lethal waste on poor nations — is receiving attention even in mainstream media. *National Geographic* and the television show *Sixty Minutes* both featured stories in 2008 on e-waste, the shipping of discarded electronics (computer monitors, cell phones) to Africa and China where people with nothing, among them many children, ruin their health and destroy the environment stripping out tiny amounts of metals and incinerating appliances in open fires to produce molten lead. And where ethics fail, self-interest sometimes succeeds. Although consumers in the United States have been happy to let transnational corporations turn China into the twenty-first century's unregulated nineteenth-century factory, some are now reviewing that blithe acquiescence as they find toxic toys in their own homes. They are beginning to understand that the poison that harms a child in China will do the same thing to a child in New Jersey. The chemical that destroys the life of a worker in the Union Carbide plant in Bhopal, India, as the activist environmental justice films *Bhopal* and *Chemical Valley* point out, will also kill workers in that company's plant in West Virginia.

Likewise, more and more people are beginning to rethink the hoarding of surplus food to trade as a commodity so that rich countries can get richer while human beings and animals starve in poor ones. Food, former president Bill Clinton publicly acknowledged at the UN in 2008, should never have been treated as just one more import/export item, just another color TV, when he was the elected leader of the United States. He specifically rued World Bank and IMF policies that make aid dependent on reduced self-sufficiency and sustainability in developing nations. Awareness of world hunger, from which no people are, in the final analysis, immune, has taught him how fundamentally wrong such a perspective is, as my own experience as the co-coordinator of a food pantry in my town in Massachusetts shows me every week. Institutionalized poverty even in the richest nation on earth insures that hunger takes a physical and spiritual toll. Elders on inadequate or no pensions, people with disabilities, working heads of families paid poverty-level wages to empty bedpans in nursing homes or clean toilets all night in office buildings, laid-off workers struggling with depression as well as poverty because of their job loss — all of these people, who are in my community black, white, Latino, and Asian, native born and immigrant, are experiencing globalization on the home front.

Also, more and more people in the United States are no longer laughing at organic food or at family or community gardens as yuppie affectations or hippie throwbacks. They realize that highly subsidized industrial agriculture in the United States as well as agricultural products from other places such as Mexico, South America, and China depend heavily on toxins that almost certainly contaminate the food. Not surprisingly, food justice has become an issue. As Barbara Kingsolver points out, U.S. factory farmers "produce 3900 calories per U.S. citizen, per day. That is twice what we need, and 700 calories a day more than they grew in 1980" (14). The obesity epidemic, now globalizing, is making people question the transnational food industry's promotion of a cheap, unhealthy diet and reflect on human beings' increasing alienation from the earth, the actual source of actual food. A growing number of people recognize the cruelty and immorality of CAFOs (concentrated animal feeding operations). Labeling contemporary free-market global economics "corporate imperialism" in an interview with Marlene Muller and Dennis Vogt in 2006, Kentucky environmentalist Wendell Berry warned more than forty years ago in "The Loss of the Future" that disaster can only come from the so-called developed world's scorn for the earth and life on it. Loss of topsoil, deforestation, annihilation of small sustainable farms, strip mining, destruction of community bonds, and disdain for the kind of deep ethics and idealism that originate in self- and earth-knowledge: all show Berry the dangerous road that late capitalism has placed us on.

More and more people are beginning to see the hypocrisy of celebrating the diverse immigrant history of the United States while branding current economic refugees criminals, especially when it is often U.S. economic and governmental policies that force people to flee poverty in their homeland. From slaughterhouses in Iowa to the fields of California that Viramontes writes about to what's left of the textile industry in North Carolina, employers are eager to hire low-paid, nonunion, undocumented workers. Many of these employers act out of nothing but greed. People afraid of deportation are not likely to quibble about work conditions, overtime pay, health benefits, or sexual harassment. But also employers often take advantage of undocumented workers' willingness to accept low wages and substandard conditions simply to stay alive in a worldwide marketplace of abysmally cheap goods and immorally cheap food made possible by globalization's exploitation of workers all over the planet. Again, this is what globalization means. What we allow to happen in other places will happen here.

ANDREW SZASZ IDENTIFIES the important environmental justice concept of inverted quarantine. By it he means the ability of the privileged to create a protected zone to keep them safe from the escalating environmental and human destruction caused by rampant economic exploitation of the earth and life on it. Drink bottled water, eat organic food, and buy only those products labeled natural, and you can insulate yourself from toxins and other contemporary hazards.

Szasz quite rightly criticizes inverted quarantine's individualized approach because it thwarts collective action. It siphons energy away from much-needed group demands for structural change. To that valuable criticism I add another: its futility. Not only is literal protection from environmental dangers impossible to achieve, as rampant cancer rates and frequent recalls of contaminated food make clear, but also no mental place of sanctuary exists. Even the idea of a safe zone is evaporating in front of people's eyes. Who today can claim not to know that unregulated capitalism is creating havoc among people and destroying the planet? Who can believe that the negative impacts will hurt only other people? Where is the safe zone? Under your bed? In the grave?

ICE raids on undocumented workers in the United States perfectly illustrate the disregard for life at the core of globalization *and* the fact that the problems cannot simply be outsourced, projected elsewhere, imagined as existing only out there/over there somewhere else — in China or South America or Africa. The disregard exists in the United States, as Jenny Alexander's film *Detained* documents. In 2008 terrorized civilian workers were set upon by armed police not somewhere in the Southern Hemisphere but in New Bedford, Massachusetts, when three hundred federal agents bombarded the manufacturing plant where immigrants sewed backpacks for U.S. soldiers in Iraq. The storm troopers arrested 360 people for not having documentation and split apart families with no provision for the welfare of children left without a parent or parents to care for them. The detained workers were bussed miles away to a military base; not long after, a number were handcuffed and flown in the middle of the night to an incarceration facility in Texas. At the time of the raid, when breast-feeding workers explained that their babies had to have their milk, ICE police herded them into a restroom, ordered them to bare their breasts, and told them to express milk to prove they were lactating. As the humiliated women did so, ICE interrogators laughed and joked with each other, asking who had the Oreo cookies to go with the milk.

This Gestapo raid did not happen in China or India or South Africa or Brazil. It happened in Massachusetts in 2008. It should not happen anywhere. And if it is permitted to happen anywhere, it will happen everywhere. Inverted quarantine may allow elites to buy their children milk free from antibiotics and added hormones and believe themselves safe. But no one is. All people's lives and the health of the planet depend, quite literally, on recognizing that the struggle for environmental justice and planetary restoration must be taken up by everyone wherever they are while we still have time to change course.

JOEL KOVEL ARGUES that capitalism cannot fix the ecological and human problems it has created. But we can. He explains in *The Enemy of Nature* that "our all-conquering capitalist system of production, the greatest and proudest of all the modalities of transforming nature which the human species has yet devised, the defining influence in modern culture and the organizer of the modern state, is at heart the enemy of nature and therefore humanity's executioner as well" (vii). The answer, he believes, is ecosocialism. He says environmental thinking wisely teaches us right relationship with the earth, but because it tends toward anarchy, it fails to offer a helpful vision of social or political organization. Socialist thought, on the other hand, offers a liberating vision of social and political democracy, one that honors the dignity and worth of all people and therefore the sharing of wealth, labor, and responsibility. But it tends to get mired in a twentieth-century obsession with class issues to the exclusion of all else and therefore fails to take ecological realities into account. Kovel merges the best of both. He links environmentalism's commitment to earth-values and sustainability with socialism's commitment to human rights and social and economic equity. His vision of ecosocialism offers tremendous hope for progressive activist reclamation of direction in the twenty-first century.

For Vine Deloria, Jr., Christianity, like capitalism, cannot fix the damaged world it has created. He says in *God Is Red* that it is not possible to "graft contemporary ecological concern" onto Christianity and expect fundamental change (292). The ground zero paradigm of Judeo-Christianity — God/man — is one of superior/inferior, dominant/subordinate, master/subject, and that hierarchical thinking inspires both the earth destruction and the human oppression that have led to the global ecological crisis the world faces today. Only by giving up basic Judeo-Christian concepts of human superiority to the rest of creation and embracing the fact that truth comes to us through visions and place-based sacred practices, not ideas and earth-detached abstractions, will human beings heal their rupture from the creation and find a living future. Whether this can and will happen Deloria does not know.

Vandana Shiva does believe that what she calls earth democracy — environmental justice and sustainable life for all — can and will be achieved if people come together as activists. Her own life spent fighting for environmental justice bears witness to the power of her faith. Trained as a physicist, she explains in *Soil Not Oil* that we can choose between two fundamental principles. One is entropic growth, which produces continued movement toward disorder and breakdown followed by increased waste, pollution, unemployment, and chaos. The other is emergent growth, the process seen in nature in which order and a meaningful arrangement of elements emerge out of disorder, as when, for example, cells multiply and form themselves into a fetus. She insists that human beings have available the most renewable source of energy on the planet: our own human energy, our capacity to think, create, change, and act. Shiva calls on us in *Soil Not Oil* to "become active agents of transformation" (135). She argues that it will not be increased technology but a return to local economies and agriculture that will rebuild human and planetary health. She commits her own life to this work of transformation because of her belief in the power of words and actions to affect the course of life on the planet.

All three of these perspectives, Kovel's, Deloria's, and Shiva's, circulate in the two brilliant, difficult, but finally extraordinarily hopeful contemporary novels with which I will end, Karen Tei Yamashita's *Tropic of Orange* and Leslie Marmon Silko's *Almanac of the Dead*.

## Heading North

You really can't separate the two in Indian Way. The political and the spiritual are one and the same. You can't believe one thing and then go out and do another. What you believe and what you do are the same thing.
— Leonard Peltier, *Prison Writings*

In *Postmodernism, or, The Cultural Logic of Late Capitalism* Fredric Jameson defines postmodernism as the philosophical or human-values manifestation of transnational global capitalism. Postmodernism's antifoundationalism, endless skepticism, and deep commitment to nihilism, often under the guise of playful irony, as if believing in nothing is just a harmless quirk of really smart people and has no consequences, mirror and in fact derive from predatory capitalism's contempt for the earth and life on it. Just as global capital disregards the truth that the planet and life itself are not simply raw material to be endlessly exploited and played with, so its cultural offspring, postmodernism, disregards the truth that truth does exist and that one paramount truth is the fact that the earth is alive and must be respected and lived with in relationship.

Published in the last decade of the twentieth century, *Tropic of Orange* and *Almanac of the Dead* prophesy the twenty-first. Each trades heavily in the idioms of postmodernism. These novels are decentered, they teem with consumer products, they enjamb time, they relish multiplicity, they collapse the sacred and profane. But they are not postmodern. Each holds fiercely at its core — its center — a set of earth-based, communal, life-affirming values. For all the terrible things each book shows, and the misery of the postmodern world abounds in both, they point us toward a living future on the planet. Like Walker and Stowe writing before abolition but knowing it must come because people *had to make it come*, like Thoreau and Hopkins insisting that environmental values and human justice *must go hand in hand*, Yamashita and Silko—like Kovel and Shiva and West and Wallis and Awiakta and many others—know that change can and will come. *If* we embrace revolution.

TROPIC OF ORANGE charts the upheaval of the postmodern world in the migration of human beings and one orange north from Mexico. Humans and food, the humans chaotically seduced/recruited/deported/discarded and the food trailing a poisonous thread from hand to hand, pull with them the invented meridian line drawn on the globe long ago by conquerors: the Tropic of Cancer. All head into the ironically and yet also, as the book unfolds, accurately named City of Angels on the Pacific Rim, a city perched near yet another artificial line drawn on the earth, this one dividing nation from nation, the United States from Mexico. Money, goods, labor, media, body parts, microbes, cars, vegetables, fear, hunger, guns, drugs, dislocation, angels, babies: all converge in Los Angeles, where Yamashita maps the urban ecology of postmodern America.

This America consists of huge numbers of homeless people. It has paved over the earth. It tolerates abysmal poverty in the midst of obscene wealth and abundance. It roars day and night with the isolated frantic transit of human beings locked inside hermetically sealed metal machines racing between yet more lines drawn on the earth—narrow, controlled little ribbons of cement, strangely dubbed "freeways." Its air glows and shimmers with toxins. Racism divides one person from another and even one from oneself, as in the case of the glamorous young woman of color, Emi, who anchors the anchorless weather in living color on TV each night and loathes multiculturalism. This America spews out traumatic stress survivors. A Japanese American surgeon turned mute following his incarceration in a U.S. internment camp during World War Two now stands naked on a freeway overpass, where he symphonically directs traffic all day. Named Manzanar (like the camp that held him), this man, we are told, is the person most at home in postmodern urban America. A domestic concentration camp survivor. A surgeon no longer healing people. A nude conductor without an orchestra wildly waving his arms above ten lanes of grinding traffic.

The contemporary urban landscape of *Tropic of Orange* is one of madness and alienation, an ecology of migrant workers, food, poisons, body organs, and souls being sucked north across the border from the South to feed the endless, rapacious appetite of the devouring metropole, a place where huge numbers of homeless people of color live under bridges and wander abandoned sidewalks. The book makes concrete Joel Kovel's point that "if humans are part of nature, then society is the human ecosystem *par excellence*; and a racist society burdened with the poverty that follows racism in every way, is a sick . . . a *disintegrating* ecosystem, one that cannot adapt to changing circumstances and heal imposed wounds" (20–21). It makes vivid Jim Wallis's insistence in *The Soul of Politics* that "the crisis of the global economy is, at root, a moral one," a crisis that reveals "the painful truth that the affluent believe their children are more important than the children of the world who are now starving to death" (84). It lays bare in dazzling postmodern detail the meaning of globalization for the earth's poor, who are overwhelmingly not white and for whom climate change, figuratively and literally, is not some future abstraction threatening dislocation, poverty, homelessness, and hunger, something dreadful heading toward humanity. It has arrived.

Paul Vallely explains in a summary of the United Nations' *Human Development Report 2007/2008* that global warming already disproportionately affects the world's poor living in the Southern Hemisphere. Monsoons and hurricanes kill and displace millions, while drought creates lifelong disadvantages for malnourished children in arid places, thereby undermining the future of entire societies. In *Soil Not Oil* Vandana Shiva connects the climate crisis and worldwide unemployment, the panic and despair of poor people unable to find work that allows them to feed their families and remain in their homes. She says that "when the rights of the poor are taken into account, there is only one way forward — reducing the energy demands of the rich and the nonsustainable patterns of production and consumption that are the legacy of industrialization and globalization" (133). The way forward, in other words, requires bringing to a halt the mad rush forward.

Yamashita's novel argues just that point. *Tropic of Orange* shows not a train wreck waiting to happen (much too nineteenth century) but a freeway pileup. And not only is that pileup waiting to happen, it *needs* to happen. Only a complete breakdown will provide the homeless with homes and the people with self-determination. A crash is needed to arrive at justice. The pileup means all traffic stops: the cars, the drugs, the organs, the toxins, the too-cheap produce from the South grown juicy on human exploitation, the media trucks blasting each evening's dose of other people's suffering into comfortable granite-countertop kitchens. Most important, as more and more thinkers now dare to propose, the pileup means the carbon stays in the earth. That is the real solution to the so-called energy crisis. Human beings in the North change how they live. They embrace a paradigm shift.

When the crash occurs in *Tropic of Orange*, when the traffic in California all screeches to a halt, the paradigm does shift. Something miraculous happens. The poor take over the abandoned cars and make a new community. They give birth to a new social order in which they repossess the manufactured and natural world — all those cars, the paved lanes, and the ignored, surrounding earth. Homeless people sleeping beneath underpasses and migrant workers afraid of deportation pour into the vacant stalled vehicles and call them home, making the symphony that Manzanar heard in his head and daily waved his arms to wish into reality materialize on the now still and actual *free*way. He was not crazy. L.A. was the crazy one.

That city, ground to a halt, now really becomes the City of Angels as characters named Gabriel, Rafaela, and Arcangel hint all along can happen. "A soft angelic quality with the repetitive chorus of the homeless encampment wafted gently above the smoking cinders of quenched fires. . . . The entire City of Angels seemed to have opened its singular voice to herald a naked old man and little boy with an orange followed by a motley parade approaching from the south" (238–39). But this angelic music of reclaimed community and emerging justice quickly turns into the "percussion of war" as U.S. armed forces gas and gun down the people. This penultimate section of the novel closes with bitter music — "Oh say can you see by the dawn's early light the rockets red glare, the bombs bursting in air?" (240) — and then, with postmodern aplomb, the book abruptly switches focus at the beginning of its final section.

That section stages a wrestling match. Instead of Ortiz's Apache and white man, into the ring step El Gran Mojado (The Great Wet-back), gorgeous in a swirling blue cape emblazoned with the Virgin of Guadalupe, and SUPERNAFTA, a Terminator-like human action figure with scorching flames springing from his head. The two give speeches, SUPERNAFTA promising the assembled poor 12 percent of the world's wealth, to which El Gran Mojado declares:

> *What can this progress my challenger speaks of*
> *really be?*
> *You who live in the declining and abandoned places*
> *of great cities, called barrios, ghettos, and favelas:*
> *What is archaic? What is modern? We are both.*
> *The myth of the first world is that*
> *development is wealth and technology progress.*
> *It is all rubbish.* (258–59)

El Gran Mojado stresses that the stakes are real: "*The life of our people or the death of our people*" (260). This wrestling match is clever, kitschy, but it is also deadly serious. The combatants kill each other. SUPER-NAFTA quite literally enacts development's role in climate change by burning to a cinder. El Gran Mojado sprouts huge white wings and billows into the heavens.

Fiercely apocalyptic, *Tropic of Orange* imagines disaster. Yet this book also insists on hope and the power of human beings to change the world. The final pages cut back to the freeway utopia, where dazed people hug and comfort one another following the government's brutal attack, and the narrative makes clear that Arcangel will not stay dead. For as Sue-Im Lee puts it, Arcangel is "a prophet and a messiah" (502). Yamashita's novel excoriates the devastation of globalization, but it does not prophesy doom. Angels in the shape of human beings —

human beings in the names of angels — tap spiritual power to transform the world. That faith in *Tropic* is never orthodox, doctrinaire, or predictable. What could be crazier than a naked Asian American surgeon turned symphonic conductor of traffic? Or a wrestler offering a socialist vision of world transformation and then wafting skyward on huge white wings? Or an orange drawing with it radical hemispheric erasure of lines that divide nations, peoples, and families? Like Apess and Walker and Stowe manipulating the dominant belief system of their time, Christianity, to call for activism in the cause of justice, so Yamashita infuses the postmodern world with ancient futuristic spirit power that is both mundane and magical. She speaks in the idiom of our time timeless truths about the power of people to reimagine and then save the world, if we will.

Jameson wishes in *Postmodernism* for the book that *Tropic of Orange* is. He knows that the answers to globalization's problems do not lie in a return to modernist values or premodern fantasies. But how might progressive political art look in the postmodern era? He theorizes that

> the new political art (if it is possible at all) will have to hold to the truth of postmodernism, that is to say, to its fundamental object — the world space of multinational capital — at the same time at which it achieves a breakthrough to some as yet unimaginable new mode of representing this last, in which we may again begin to grasp our positioning as individual and collective subjects and regain a capacity to act and struggle which is at present neutralized by our spatial as well as our social confusion. (54)

Set in the world space of multinational capital, *Tropic* offers a vision of progressive political activism. In an interview with Jean Vengua Gier and Carla Alicia Tejada, Yamashita explains that she did not set herself the task of rendering postmodernity, but she did know she was writing a deeply political book and refused to compromise on its message. As she puts it, "In 1991, when I began this project about Los Angeles, about the movement of the Tropic of Cancer into Los Angeles, and was trying to articulate it on the page in a very experimental, non-conventional way (which I insisted on doing), it could not be published in any other venue except a small press like Coffee House. They were the only press who would accept that project. Any other conventional press found it too experimental and didn't want the politics." She adds: "In 1991, if you had said I was doing a 'postmodern project,' I'd have thought, 'What the hell is that?'" But since then, she notes, the conversation has interested her.

My students love *Tropic of Orange*. They instantly recognize the narrative's overlapping perspectives, multiraciality, simultaneous geographies, crisscrosses of lines, superfluity of stuff, endless traffic, and sane insanity/insane sanity as their world. Its mapping of urban ecology, use of postmodern idioms, and critique of globalization resonate powerfully with them. But above all they welcome and embrace its deeply unpostmodern magical realist vision of a new and different world order: one in which angels exist ("not 'out there' somewhere," as one student wrote in her journal, "but in communities"); where lines on the earth drawn by strangers come to life and move of their own accord; and where the battle between NAFTA and undocumented immigrant workers literally takes place — but on a level playing field: SUPERNAFTA versus El Gran Mojado. As one student wrote of the novel in his journal, "It seems chaotic but there *is* connection and pattern." Another said, deliberately ending with an ellipsis: "There *is* meaning in this book, even if it is fractured — which is the point. . . ." The novel exposes, prophesies, inspires. And then leaves the work to us.

I ALWAYS END my course on environmental justice and U.S. literature with an all-class activism project conceived, organized, and carried out by the students, the purpose of which is multiple. The project puts into practice the truth that human beings have agency and that activism in the service of progressive change is an important goal of the liberal tradition in the humanities. It allows students to experience the value of working collectively to achieve a common end. And it deprivatizes their learning by having them teach what they have learned to others. I offer guidelines on how to avoid pitfalls such as unequal participation or unrealistic timelines, but after that I never know what they will do. I simply show up when and where they tell me to see what they have created.

Three years ago the class of twenty used *Tropic of Orange* as their inspiration. On a hundred tiny pieces of paper they wrote facts about environmental injustice — what it is, how it operates, how it saturates the food we eat daily, how it shows its global face, what people can do to bring about change — and attached each slip of paper to a toothpick stuck in an orange. They assembled in front of the university library and handed the toothpick-festooned oranges to students, faculty, visitors, and staff who walked by, saying to each: "Please read before you enjoy the orange." A third of the way into their demonstration, with about half of their oranges gone and their spirits high because of the generally positive reception, a large crowd of preteens on a campus visit from our local urban middle school poured onto the library patio. In the space of five minutes the twelve-year-olds had accepted every last orange and disappeared shrieking and dancing around the corner of the building.

At first my stunned students, with an hour left to fill and not one orange, started to ask each other why they had wasted their oranges on kids; they should have saved them for fellow students and other adults. But then they started to wonder. The paper-flagged toothpicks were leaving campus. Some would show up in kitchens across town of families with ancestors in the United States for a hundred years or more, others in kitchens of new immigrants who might have documentation papers or might not. Some toothpick messages would get thrown in the trash unread or make no sense when read, but others would start a conversation, resonate with an adult's experience, or plant the seed of an idea in a child's mind. The students decided that the unexpected disappearance of their oranges to places they could not completely visualize, unlike their professors' offices or friends' dormitory rooms, was perfect, as was the laughter that now overcame them when they thought about the preteens' zany energy. As Michael Albert argues in *The Trajectory of Change*, and they now agreed was really true, activism needs to be joyful — even fun — at times as well as earnest, courageous, and tireless. Certainly, they decided, it fit well with *Tropic of Orange* that kids walked away with more than half of the oranges.

## Climate Change

Where Native peoples are placed within the current global political economy has significant ramifications not only for Native peoples but for all peoples interested in social justice.
—Andrea Smith, *Native Americans and the Christian Right*

It took Leslie Marmon Silko ten years to write *Almanac of the Dead*, of which she stated: "This is my 763 page indictment for five hundred years of theft, murder, pillage, and rape." The huge, profoundly disturbing novel, which the Laguna Pueblo author has also described as "a moral history of America from a Native American point of view," details where five hundred years of Western colonialism have brought the world.

Radiating in all directions from Tucson, Arizona, *Almanac of the Dead* has six parts: "The United States of America," "Mexico," "Africa," "The Americas," "The Fifth World," "One World, Many Tribes." Together they record the so-called progress of the modern world. Uranium mining slices off mesas and dumps toxic waste in mammoth radio active tailings. Poor women in the Southern Hemisphere abandon newborns in trash cans while children in the North, of which there are almost none, disappear. Torture videos, sadomasochistic pornography, drugs of every sort, and high-powered automatic weapons command lucrative global markets. Rich retirees build golf courses and canals in the Arizona desert that drain millions of gallons of water from underground aquifers while undocumented workers from Mexico die of dehydration trying to cross the border to find work. Israel forgets its own people's past as it confines Palestinians in concentration camps in their own homeland, making, as one character puts it, Hitler smile. A thriving international trade in body parts from living donors in poor nations stocks Western hospitals and laboratories with human flesh to save the rich and satisfy the curiosity of scientists. Hollywood moguls film holy places on the earth that indigenous people have asked them not to violate. And artificial biospheres are in the works to provide elites with a new habitat once the planet Earth has been destroyed.

This terrifying picture is not science fiction. Silko — like Apess, Walker, Stowe, Viramontes, Ortiz, and countless other progressive activist writers — simply tells the truth. As Kari Lydersen reports, scientists now warn that waterborne diseases are increasing enormously because of global warming. As Modhumita Roy describes, destitute women in India in the early twenty-first century agree to rent their wombs to infertile elites from around the world and then live under lock and key in group facilities as virtual prisoners while implanted embryos grow in their uteruses. As Verlyn Klinkenborg explains, the disappearance of darkness in the developed world due to huge patches of the earth being illuminated all night has disastrous effects on birds and other animals. As Billy Baker notes, 27 percent of the species that Thoreau documented at Walden Pond only 150 years ago are gone and another 36 percent will soon disappear. As I saw for myself, along forested roads in Uganda soldiers stand guard to prevent the poor from harvesting wood to use as fuel or sell because they have no other livelihood. In Nigeria, as Abayomi Azikiwe records, Royal Dutch Shell and the government make large profits from oil extraction that has completely destroyed and polluted the entire Niger Delta ecosystem. Nothing can grow there anymore because the soil and groundwater are poisonous, and the impoverished population suffers massive disease and illness.

Perhaps most terrible is the patenting of seeds by transnational corporations in a practice known as biopiracy or biocolonialism. Agrochemical corporations modify in some tiny way seeds developed by farmers for generations and then patent them to make them the corporation's sole property. Next, to secure the market, industry scientists implant terminator technology. "This genetically engineered technology ensures that a seed injected with the 'suicide gene' does not germinate after harvesting," explains the 2004 Nobel Peace Prize winner and founder of the Green Belt Movement in Kenya, Wangari Maathai. "This means the farmers will have to buy seed each season, and cannot develop their own seed" (2).

In *Recovering the Sacred* Winona LaDuke documents such patenting of wild rice, the Anishinaabe people's traditional food for more than a thousand years in what is now Minnesota. Ken Foster and Zan Hua Zahn of the Nor-Cal Wild Rice Corporation in California hold the patent. "How the hell could they do that?" LaDuke reports Native people exclaiming. "After all, the Creator gave *manoomin* to the Anishinaabeg, not Norcal" (177). Added to moral outrage is very real fear. If the rice with the terminator gene mingles with rice that has not been mutilated, the gene could easily infect the entire crop, leaving only the engineered product and forcing everyone to buy it. If blight were to wipe out that strain, the rice itself would disappear. As Maathai observes of this at the global level, "Under these circumstances, if we thought that slavery and colonialism were gross violations of human rights, we have to wake up to what is awaiting us down the secretive road of biopiracy, patenting of life and genetic engineering. Genocide from hunger, such as we have not yet seen, becomes a haunting possibility" (2).

ONE WAY OF understanding *Almanac of the Dead* is this. It presents terminator gene mentality as the moral norm of the postmodern world. It shows that producing death is the primary mission of contemporary globalization, the logical outcome of five hundred years of Western colonial exploitation of the earth and brutal domination of native peoples, beginning with genocide in the Americas and enslavement of Africans. Suicide is what the Western world is embarked upon. Self-amputation from the creation.

Should it be surprising, then, that the latest intellectual plaything of sophisticated postmodernity is the death of nature? Joining the post-race/gender/nation/colonialism hoax today is postnature. Explaining that he is not a postmodernist but is a deconstructionist and that he does take seriously global warming, Timothy Morton states in *Ecology without Nature*: "the very idea of 'nature' which so many hold so dear . . .

is getting in the way of proper ecological forms of culture, philosophy, politics, and art" (1). He argues that nature has become a meaningless signifier. The important thing for us to do, therefore, is not act but, rather, correct this theoretical misconception, which he does in detail. Patricia Yaeger discusses art photos and contemporary literary celebrations of debris in the developed world in "The Death of Nature and the Apotheosis of Trash; or, Rubbish Ecology," published in literary criticism's most prestigious journal, *PMLA*. The elegant essay reads trash as the sublime in elite postmodern art. Only in a parenthetical aside does the discussion raise the possibility that some might take issue with aestheticizing rich people's waste in a world where toxins are poisoning the poor.

Foreseeing this alienation perfectly in *Almanac*, Silko foregrounds two brilliant pieces of postmodern art. One is a series of photographs of a suicide, the body artfully manipulated by means of double exposures into a complicated composition of colors and blossoms made up of flowers and blood. Critics' ecstatic reception rewards the photographer's careful positioning of light sources so that the suicide's skin glistens amid the tumbling flowers. "One critic wrote of the 'pictorial irony of a field of red shapes which might be peonies — cherry, ruby, deep purple, black — and the nude human figure nearly buried in these 'blossoms' of bright red" (108). Or, the reader reflects, the red shapes might be human blood and a person dead in his twenties. But never mind. Gorgeous trash in the developed world — whether suicide victims or mountains of rubbish — all serves the slick aesthetic of cynicism that postmodern fundamentalism worships. As Jameson remarks, "Postmodernism is what you have when the modernization process is complete and nature is gone for good" (ix).

Displaying that truth, *Almanac*'s other prominent example of postmodern aesthetics is a stunning mansion commissioned by the Mexican capitalist Menardo. Costing millions, the fabulous palace in the jungle mimics the Aztec pyramids in shape but, in an obvious joke on Silko's part, uses glass for each external wall. Symbol of Menardo's hubris, it is a huge fragile monument to his misguided faith in inverted quarantine. Others may have to worry about stones being thrown, bullets flying, contaminants being present, the poor taking revenge, but not Menardo. He is insulated, safe. He wears a bulletproof vest at all times, even when he sleeps. But the glass house, like the postmodernity it refracts into the dense living jungle and the rapacious greed it flaunts, is all surface; it has no depth, no secure grounding or roots in the earth, no protective power. The narrative plays with the well-known adage that people who live in glass houses should not throw stones. *Almanac's* revision of that truism might read: global capitalists who exploit the poor and poison the planet should watch their backs.

WHILE WRITING *Almanac of the Dead,* Silko explains in "Notes from the Author," she took time out to spray paint activist messages about a political issue on the wall opposite her small office in a rundown part of Tucson. Then, when the issue was resolved, to thank fellow residents for putting up with her graffiti she painted over her words a huge gentle snake with its belly full of skulls. Above the snake she wrote these words in Spanish on her forty-foot mural: "The people are hungry. The people are cold. The rich have stolen the land. The rich have stolen freedom. The people demand justice. Otherwise, Revolution."

Revolution propels *Almanac.*

Silko's novel insists that indigenous values and beliefs have not been extinguished by five hundred years of conquest. Resistance has been constant throughout those centuries. Truth still comes to Native

Americans in dreams and visions. The great Apache warrior Geronimo and the great Paiute prophet Wovoka have not been forgotten. The ancient sacred serpent beings Quetzalcoatl and Damballah, demonized by Western religion but understood as sources of strength and power by indigenous peoples on both sides of the Atlantic, still live. The spirit macaws continue to speak. Pages of the ancient Mayan almanac survive, even if in fragments, to guide the battle for liberation.

*Almanac of the Dead* labels Christianity a lethal force in the Americas. As soon as the invaders pledged themselves to genocide, slavery, and religious intolerance — the insistence that only they had the truth — Christianity identified itself as a cannibal, one of the Destroyers. Its sacrament of eating human flesh and drinking blood makes it no secret.

Marxism, by contrast, appeals to the revolutionary Angelita La Escapía. Marx "was the first white man La Escapía had ever heard call his own people vampires and monsters." She reads his descriptions of "the tiny corpses of children who had been worked to death — their deformed bodies shaped to fit inside factory machinery and other cramped spaces" — and sees his analysis confirmed all around her in Mexico City's unbreathable air and screaming traffic. She "laughed out loud. This was the end of what the white man had to offer the Americas: poison smog in the winter and the choking clouds that swirled off sewage treatment leaching fields and filled the sky with fecal dust in early spring. Here was the place Marx had in mind as 'a place of human sacrifice, a shrine where thousands passed yearly through the fire as offerings to the Moloch of avarice'" (312–13). Yet Marx is not saying anything that tribal people did not already know, La Escapía recognizes. His voice simply joins those of Geronimo, Wovoka, the unnamed leaders of slave revolts, the American Indian warriors who refused conversion, the Native grandmothers who saved the pages of the ancient almanacs and appear on the first page of Silko's new one stirring up revolution on a kitchen stove outside Tucson, Arizona, on the brink of the twenty-first century.

The future of the planet does not depend on Jesus or Marx. It depends on relearning our relationship to the earth.

ALMANACS PROPHESY. They collect information and give advice. Often they foretell the future: how to see it now, how to plan, how to avoid disaster and bring about health and plenty.

Earth-based almanacs predict the weather, tell us when to plant seeds so that they will grow and when to harvest. They deliver this wisdom by knowing the past — history — and understanding the mysteries of the creation, the way that forces visible and invisible come together to support life on earth. They do not proceed by means of logical argument or sustained flowing narrative. Rather, they place side by side pieces and bits of knowledge, even small fragments, that may not at first seem related but the accumulation of which over space and time generates coherence and a clear picture. Read over and over, even entered randomly, dipped into here or there, they communicate with their readers and listeners in an ancient, nonlinear way that resonates with the truth that all life connects in endless repeated patterns — cycles, circles, webs — none of them a straight line.

All of this describes Silko's *Almanac*. The novel prophesies the disappearance of white people from the Americas, the rebellion of the earth's poor, and the survival of the planet, with or without human beings. As one of the twentieth century's great war novels, which it is, *Almanac of the Dead* forecasts the future. Activism will surge in the Americas. A multiracial army of the homeless will be led by a black Vietnam War veteran. Ecowarriors will give their lives for the earth. Fierce Ghost Dancers will lead the material and spiritual revolution that must come if the globe is to be freed from its current death-wish born of centuries of Western colonialism, including contemporary globalization. And the earth will be freed. Of that *Almanac of the Dead* is certain. The question — which is also the reason for hope in this brutally honest book, which, like all almanacs, is meant to be *used* — is this: will human beings recognize that the earth is sacred and change their relationship to all life in the creation while there is still time to do so? Silko knows the earth will live regardless. Humans will not.

ALMANAC OF THE DEAD disturbs the most basic Western concepts of power. After my students read the first third, they come in excited, overwhelmed, but sure of their task. Most have started to develop elaborate character lists and diagrams charting episodes and timelines. By the second week, many start to abandon those lists and charts; the book is too big and resists control. By the final week, almost all of them simply read, moving with the narrative wherever it goes, without lists, charts, or other attempts at mastery. They accept a way of knowing and seeing that draws on Western practices — words on the page written in English — but also invokes methods of comprehending that are not familiar. In *Almanac* narratives appear and disappear; time moves in all directions; spirits speak; fiction intermingles with history; languages, beings, and beliefs tap readers' existing knowledge and others elude or surprise. One begins to realize the novel expresses the principles of the earth — repetition, circularity, innovation, interrelation — and participates in an aesthetic that is fierce and abundant but radically anticolonial. The usual methods of Western interpretation, whether tidy (even if complex) linear exposition of meaning or indecisive brilliant deconstruction upon deconstruction rendered from a superior vantage point, do not work. *Almanac* demands humility and courage, the kind of deep thinking that Awiakta names walking in one's soul. The novel asks for transformation. It confronts readers with the necessity of *action*.

## The Paradigm of Hope

The lands of the planet call to humankind for redemption.
—Vine Deloria, Jr., *God Is Red*

Jim Wallis says in *God's Politics*, "The choice between cynicism and hope is ultimately a spiritual choice, one that has enormous political consequences" (346), and every text I have discussed confirms that truth, from Apess, Walker, and Stowe refusing despair more than a century and a half ago to Viramontes and Ortiz and Silko doing the same today. The liberal activist tradition in U.S. literature — from before Apess to Yamashita to writers not yet published — insists that the people can change the world.

As a faith system, global capital maintains that everything can be bought and sold. Nothing is off limits. Not women's wombs, not water, not new life in a seed, not space, not sacred mesas, not childhood, not animal relatives, not even the weather, increasingly thrown into chaos in the twenty-first century by rampant consumption of carbon. As Joel Kovel says, "Capital, money-in-action, becomes both a kind of intoxicating god, and also . . . a 'force field' polarizing our relation to nature in such a way that spells disaster. From being the creature of nature we have become capital's puppet" (5). Thoreau warned of that 150 years ago, Hopkins 100 years ago, Robinson 30 years ago, and Yamashita and Silko yesterday. But each also reminds us that we can cut the puppet strings. We can, in fact, throw off the puppet master.

Kovel explains that the goal is to build a free society. He prophesies that, although the ecological crisis will continue to produce terrible suffering and damage for a period of time, human beings will make deep changes by the end of the twenty-first century. "The shape this takes will entail the replacement of Lord Capital by a more ecologically rational way of production. Of that I am quite certain" (25), he states.

For Michael Lerner two basic possibilities exist, the paradigm of fear and the paradigm of hope. Along with Wallis, Kovel, Awiakta, West, LaDuke, Shiva, and many others, he emphasizes that progressive people have a choice. We can embrace despair and nihilism. We can consider all assertions of truth illegitimate, the domain of the weak-minded and/or brainwashed, and label stupid or dangerous any serious contemplation of spiritual values. I have argued that academic humanists too often do that today. Most liberal humanists inside and outside academic settings rightly regard religious fundamentalism as the enemy of human freedom and equality and of the earth's health. Religious fundamentalism shuts down open inquiry, thinking for oneself, and nonauthoritarian ways of living on the planet. It epitomizes Lerner's paradigm of fear, a view of the world that believes in divinely ordained systems of hierarchy, law, order, and control that must be obeyed on pain of eternal damnation. Yet many liberal humanists replace that paradigm of fear with one of their own.

Postmodern fundamentalism's commitment to endless critique-for-its-own-sake, critique amputated from activism and even contemptuous of it, as if pointing out everything that is wrong without attention to or belief in the power of human beings to enact progressive change tells the whole story, frequently defines humanist thought today, especially in the academy. The basis of this worldview is fear: conviction that people have neither the capacity nor the will to change the world. But as Lerner and others such as Winona LaDuke, Awiakta, Scott Russell Sanders, and Cornel West stress, fear is not the only paradigm available, as U.S. history shows, from the struggle for abolition two hundred years ago to the election of Barack Obama as president of the nation at the beginning of the twenty-first century. Its alternative is the paradigm of hope. That paradigm believes human beings have the power to create fundamental positive change and will take action in the service of social justice and planetary health.

The paradigm of hope shapes the liberal activist tradition in American literature. I have pointed to a very small number of texts in this tradition — Apess's "Looking-Glass for the White Man," Walker's *Appeal*, a group of Chinese merchants' letters to the editor, Stowe's *Uncle Tom's Cabin*, Thoreau's *Walden* and antislavery works, Hopkins's *Winona*, Ortiz's *Men on the Moon*, Robinson's *Housekeeping*, Viramontes's *Under the Feet of Jesus*, Naylor's *Mama Day*, Yamashita's *Tropic of Orange*, Silko's *Almanac of the Dead*. Each offers a sobering view of human abuse of the gift of life. These literary works confirm the fact that the issues facing progressive activists have always been dire, as they are today. Yet each insists that human beings have the ability to make a different world. Refusing hopelessness, each has faith in the people's willingness to listen, learn, and be changed. Despite postmodernism's love affair with skepticism and nihilism, the liberal activist tradition in American literature testifies to the truth that words do have the power to strengthen and inspire people in the activist struggle to heal the world.

Pessimism is hard to fend off in our time — just as it was for the abolitionists and as it has always been for people fighting for Indian sovereignty, women's rights, gay and lesbian equality, true economic justice, racial equity, and religious freedom. The struggle for environmental justice and restoration of the earth requires profound changes, especially on the part of people in the United States. It is not a matter of continuing on our present course, Newt Gingrich's right-wing notion of entrepreneurial environmentalism notwithstanding. And the practical arguments of concerned liberals such as Ted Nordhaus and George Monbiot that we can somehow simply green-up our current bloated way of life are not much more realistic. As Val Plumwood emphasizes, "techno-optimist scenarios" (6) miss the point. The resource-drunk North must change, literally and spiritually. That is why the humanities are crucial. Postmodern fundamentalism's angst and nihilism have driven some who care deeply about other people and the earth, including a number of ecocritics, to retreat into doomsday despair. Others have made the unwise decision to give up on the humanities in favor of acquiring scientific environmental knowledge in order to be legitimate. But as many people have explained, Western science practices the very alienated reasoning that has led us to believe human beings can and should conquer and control nature. I was shocked to hear a speaker at a recent conference say to a room of nodding humanists that the cost to society of an incompetent doctor is higher than the cost to society of an incompetent English professor. In fact, the cost of the latter is infinitely higher. Humanists, inside and outside academic settings, need to be saying that — loudly. What we are forgetting are the very lessons of the past that progressive people cherish: activist struggle is not easy, but it is mandatory, and it *does* work.

In my experience many young people are open to this message of hope. Robert Figueroa and Steve Chase explain that students welcome the units on activism in the courses they teach. I find the same thing.

As one person in my Environmental Justice and U.S. Literature class in 2008 commented about the group's final social activism project, "I now realize I myself do not have to be the 'hero' or the 'savior,' that there is a value in collective action and alliances and that confusion about how to solve the problem will not suffice to justify non-action and apathy." Another reflected: "[What] I wish to retain is the call to action. Learning about injustice or even learning about others' struggles to bring about change is ineffective without also taking action yourself." The student asked by his peers to construct four ten-foot-tall skull-and-crossbones-emblazoned smokestacks to anchor the class's social action wrote: "For me, I honestly thought nobody would care even to inquire about our project. That is why I set out to make the smoke stacks as large and gaudy as possible in an attempt to garner some query from passersby. It worked, and that surprised me the most. People actually are interested."

The paradigm of hope knows what the students discovered. People actually are interested. Not everyone. But enough to build a different future. At a colloquium in 2007 the Northern Cheyenne visual artist Bently Spang spoke about the long, terrible history of genocide against indigenous peoples in the Americas. But he also shared his belief that a new willingness to learn and change was taking place at the grassroots level. He did not see top-level U.S. leaders at that time moving away from old hatreds and closed-mindedness. But at the grassroots, among the young especially, he saw change, a desire to learn and to see differently.

Vine Deloria, Jr., says at the end of *God Is Red*:

Who will find peace with the lands? The future of humankind lies waiting for those who will come to understand their lives and take up their responsibilities to all living things. Who will listen to the trees, the animals and birds, the voices of the places of the land? As the long-forgotten peoples of the respective continents rise and begin to reclaim their ancient heritage, they will discover the meaning of the lands of their ancestors. That is when the invaders of the North American continent will finally discover that for this land, God is red. (296)

Revolution will come. From Apess to Silko, Walker to Yamashita, Stowe to Ortiz, that has been the message of the liberal activist literary tradition in America. The struggle of justice against oppression, hope against despair, is hard. But it has long been the work of humanists, and of literature in particular, to put before the world *both* terms in each of those dyads — justice as well as oppression, hope as well as despair — to help people commit to the first in each case.

Vandana Shiva writes of the daunting task we face today in *Soil Not Oil*. Yet she believes we can as human beings reorient our values and reorganize how we live, "making the impossible possible, creating hope out of hopelessness, unleashing our creative energies in the midst of ecological and social ruin" (142). It is out of fashion to say this, but it is nonetheless true: liberal activist texts have transformative power. They play a profound role in the fight for human justice and planetary healing that so many of us recognize as the urgent struggle of our own time. Words on the page reach more than our minds. They call up our feelings. They call out our spirits. They can move us to act.

THE LAST SECTION of *Almanac of the Dead* is titled "ONE WORLD, MANY TRIBES." Its first and only book: "PROPHECY."

*Almanac's* prophecy, at once frightening and hope inspiring, foretells this future: tribal peoples and the poor will retake the earth, and the living planet — with or without human beings — will not die. Courageous messengers bring these truths. A Lakota poet-lawyer and self-taught healer born forty miles from where the people were massacred at Wounded Knee, Wilson Weasel Tail, quotes Pontiac and the great Paiute prophet Wovoka, to whom the Ghost Dance came in a vision. With rage as profound as William Apess's and as scorching as David Walker's, he indicts "the white man's law. The law crushed and cheated the poor whatever color they were" (714). This Lakota prophet declares, "All that is left is the power of poetry," and reveals, "The spirits are outraged! They demand justice! The spirits are furious! To all those humans too weak or too lazy to protect Mother Earth, the spirits say, 'Too bad you did not die fighting the destroyers of the earth because now *we* will kill you for being so weak, for wringing your hands and whimpering while the invaders committed outrages against the forest and the mountains'" (714, 723). He voices the truth repeated often in indigenous America: "The Ghost Dance has never ended, it has continued" (724).

The black Vietnam vet leader of the Army of the Homeless, Clinton, realizes: "Nothing could be black only or brown only or white only anymore. The ancient prophecies had foretold a time when the destruction by man had left the earth desolate, and the human race was itself endangered. This was the last chance the people had against the Destroyers, and they would never prevail if they did not work together as a common force" (747).

The militant revolutionary Angelita La Escapía recognizes: "Now it was up to the poorest tribal people and survivors of European genocide to show the remaining humans how all could share and live together on earth, ravished as she was" (749).

The international organizer of tribal peoples known as the Barefoot Hopi extols contemporary ecowarriors willing to die for the earth and forecasts radical global shifts in population that will totally redistribute power.

These prophecies in *Almanac* are dark. Violence and pain will precede restoration of human beings' right relation to the earth and to each other, with neither outcome guaranteed. The future foreseen is not sweet or easy. Yet hope persists. The poor and dark skinned, the disenfranchised and dispossessed, are on the move. The earth will endure.

HARRIET BEECHER STOWE 150 years ago said she had to write *Uncle Tom's Cabin*. So too, on the brink of the twenty-first century, Leslie Marmon Silko knew no peace until her manuscript was complete. As Kimberly Robollo notes, Silko told a friend that the "spirits rode her" (543) until the last word of *Almanac of the Dead* was on the page.

ONE OF MY STUDENTS who gave up a law career to return to college to train as a high school teacher sent me this e-mail in 2008 while student teaching in a working-class town near Boston.

> At an English teacher lunch last Thursday, I casually asked the other teachers what they normally did for Martin Luther King Day. Not surprisingly, everyone looked at me like I was crazy — didn't I know that MLK day had fallen into the same bowl of oatmeal as holidays for dead presidents? — i.e., please shut up and enjoy your time off! Notwithstanding that reaction, I gathered quotes from Eugene Debs, Frederick Douglass, Oscar Wilde, Pauline Hopkins, and Martin Luther King, Jr., and read them to start my classes off Friday morning. It was a big hit — with some students responding by saying that "teachers don't usually think of us as agents of change."

What the next generation believes possible does matter.

# Acknowledgment

Some people knew they helped me as I wrote this book, but some did not know. I am very grateful to Mark Ammons, Missouri Ammons, Chiyo Crawford, Kathy Fast, Deborah Horvitz, Joycelyn Moody, Hank Peirce, David Pinckney, Modhumita Roy, Christina Sharpe, everyone at the Community Cupboard, fellow workers on the Immigration Task Force, and all my students. I also want to thank my terrific editor at Iowa, Holly Carver. For a Senior Faculty Research Grant and excellent library assistance, I am happy to acknowledge my university, Tufts.

# A Note on Method

Instead of foot- or endnotes, I provide in the works cited my sources for all the ideas of others to which I refer as well as for direct quotations, which I keep to a minimum. I have consciously chosen this method because I want this book to be broadly accessible. Also, I don't believe that the writing of academic humanists needs to be as laden with notes, especially dense talky ones that create a virtual parallel text, as has become the habit today.

# Works Cited

Adamson, Joni, and Scott Slovic, eds. *Ethnicity and Ecocriticism.* Spec. issue of *MELUS: Multi-Ethnic Literature of the United States* 34 (Summer 2009).

Albert, Michael. *The Trajectory of Change: Activist Strategies for Social Transformation.* Boston: South End, 2002.

Ammons, Elizabeth. "Freeing the Slaves and Banishing the Blacks: Racism, Empire, and Africa in *Uncle Tom's Cabin.*" *Harriet Beecher Stowe's* Uncle Tom's Cabin*: A Casebook.* Ed. Elizabeth Ammons. New York: Oxford UP, 2007. 227–46.

———. "Heroines in *Uncle Tom's Cabin.*" *American Literature* 49 (May 1980): 161–79.

Angelou, Maya. *Poems.* New York: Bantam, 1997.

Apess, William. *On Our Own Ground: The Complete Writings of William Apess, a Pequot.* Ed. Barry O'Connell. Amherst: U of Massachusetts P, 1992.

Armstrong, Karen. *The Battle for God: A History of Fundamentalism.* New York: Random House, 2001.

———. *The Great Transformation: The Beginning of Our Religious Traditions.* New York: Alfred A. Knopf, 2006.

Awiakta, Marilou. *Selu: Seeking the Corn-Mother's Wisdom*. Golden, CO: Fulcrum Publishing, 1993.

Azikiwe, Abayomi. "Higher Oil Prices Breed Repression." *Workers World* 2 Oct. 2008: 11.

Baker, Billy. "Troubling Toll in Thoreau's Backyard." *Boston Globe* 28 Oct. 2008: A7c, B6.

Baldwin, James. "Everybody's Protest Novel." *Partisan Review* 16 (June 1949): 578–85.

Belasco, Susan. Introduction. *Stowe in Her Own Time: A Biographical Chronicle of Her Life, Drawn from Recollections, Interviews, and Memoirs by Family, Friends, and Associates*. Ed. Susan Belasco. Iowa City: U of Iowa P, 2008. xi–xxxvi.

Bello, Walden. "Global Economic Counterrevolution: The Dynamics of Impoverishment and Marginalization." *Toxic Struggles: The Theory and Practice of Environmental Justice*. Ed. Richard Hofrichter. Salt Lake City: U of Utah P, 2002. 197–208.

Berman, Russell A. "The Humanities, Globalization, and the Transformation of the University." *ADE Bulletin* 144 (Winter 2008): 26–30.

Berry, Wendell. *A Continuous Harmony: Essays Cultural and Agricultural*. Washington, DC: Shoemaker & Hoard, 1970.

———. *Life Is a Miracle: An Essay against Modern Superstition*. Washington, DC: Counterpoint, 2000.

*Bhopal: The Search for Justice*. Dir. Lindalee Tracey and Peter Raymont. White Pine Pictures and the National Film Board of Canada, 2004.

Brodkin, Karen. *How Jews Became White Folks and What That Says about Race in America*. New Brunswick, NJ: Rutgers UP, 1998.

Brown, Lois. *Pauline Elizabeth Hopkins: Black Daughter of the Revolution*. Chapel Hill: U of North Carolina P, 2008.

Buell, Lawrence. *Writing for an Endangered World: Literature, Culture, and Environment in the U.S. and Beyond*. Cambridge, MA: Harvard UP, 2001.

Bullard, Robert D., ed. *Confronting Environmental Racism: Voices from the Grassroots*. Boston: South End, 1993.

Butler, Judith, Ernest Laclau, and Slavoj Žižek. *Contingency, Hegemony, Universality: Contemporary Dialogues on the Left*. London: Verso, 2000.

Cannon, Katie Geneva. *Katie's Canon: Womanism and the Soul of the Black Community.* New York: Continuum, 1995.

Cervantes, Lorna Dee. *Emplumada.* Pittsburgh, PA: U of Pittsburgh P, 1981.

Chase, Steve. "Changing the Nature of Environmental Studies: Teaching Environmental Justice to 'Mainstream' Students." *The Environmental Justice Reader: Politics, Poetics, and Pedagogy.* Ed. Joni Adamson, Mei Mei Evans, and Rachel Stein. Tucson: U of Arizona P, 2002. 350–67.

*Chemical Valley.* Dir. Mimi Pickering and Anne Lewis Johnson. Headwaters and Appalshop, 1991.

Child, Lydia Maria. *Letters of Lydia Maria Child, with a Biographical Introduction by John G. Whittier and an Appendix by Wendell Phillips.* Boston: Houghton Mifflin, 1883.

Chow, Rey. *Ethics after Idealism: Theory — Culture — Ethnicity — Reading.* Bloomington: Indiana UP, 1998.

Christian, Barbara. "The Race for Theory." *Cultural Critique* 6 (Spring 1987): 51–63.

Cone, James H. *Risks of Faith: The Emergence of a Black Theology of Liberation, 1968–1998.* Boston: Beacon, 1999.

———. *Speaking the Truth: Ecumenism, Liberation, and Black Theology.* Grand Rapids, MI: William B. Eerdmans, 1986.

Cook-Lynn, Elizabeth. *Notebooks of Elizabeth Cook-Lynn.* Tucson: U of Arizona P, 2007.

Crenshaw, Kimberle, Neil Gotanda, Gary Peller, and Kendall Thomas, eds. *Critical Race Theory: The Key Writings That Formed the Movement.* New York: New Press, 1995.

Dawkins, Richard. *The God Delusion.* New York: Houghton Mifflin, 2006.

Deloria, Vine, Jr. *God Is Red.* 1973. New York: Grosset & Dunlap, 2003.

———. "Vision and Community: A Native American Voice." *Native and Christian: Indigenous Voices on Religious Identity in the United States and Canada.* Ed. James Treat. New York: Routledge, 1996. 105–14.

*Detained: The New Bedford Immigration Raid.* Dir. Jenny Alexander. Western Massachusetts Coalition for Immigrant and Worker Rights, 2008.

*DJ Spooky's Rebirth of a Nation.* Dir. Paul D. Miller. Starz Media, 2008.

Dyer, Richard. "The Matter of Whiteness." *Theories of Race and Racism: A Reader.* Ed. Les Back and John Solomos. New York: Routledge, 2000. 539–48.

Ferrante, Joan, and Prince Browne, Jr. *The Social Construction of Race and Ethnicity in the United States.* 2nd ed. Upper Saddle Road, NJ: Prentice Hall, 2001.

Figueroa, Robert. "Teaching for Transformation: Lessons from Environmental Justice." *The Environmental Justice Reader: Politics, Poetics, and Pedagogy.* Ed. Joni Adamson, Mei Mei Evans, and Rachel Stein. Tucson: U of Arizona P, 2002. 311–30.

Fish, Stanley. Blog. "Politics and the Classroom: One More Try." 8 June 2008. Web.

Frankenberg, Ruth. *White Women, Race Matters: The Social Construction of Whiteness.* Minneapolis: U of Minnesota P, 1993.

Freire, Paulo. *Teachers as Cultural Workers: Letters to Those Who Dare Teach.* Trans. Donaldo Macedo, Dale Koike, and Alexandre Oliveira. Boulder, CO: Westview, 2005.

Gates, Henry Louis, Jr., gen. ed. *The Schomburg Library of Nineteenth-Century Black Women Writers.* New York: Oxford UP, 1988, 1991.

Gier, Jean Vengua, and Carla Alicia Tejada. *An Interview with Karen Tei Yamashita.* 1998. Web. http://social.chass.ncsu.edu/jouvert/v2i2/hamashi.htm.

Gingrich, Newt, and Terry L. Maple. *A Contract with the Earth.* New York: Penguin, 2008.

Gitlin, Todd. *The Twilight of Our Common Dreams.* New York: Metropolitan Books, 1995.

Glotfelty, Cheryll, and Harold Fromm, eds. *The Ecocriticism Reader: Landmarks in Literary Ecology.* Athens: U of Georgia P, 1996.

Gossett, Thomas F. Uncle Tom's Cabin *and American Culture.* Dallas, TX: Southern Methodist UP, 1985.

Grewe-Volpp, Christa. "'The oil was made from their bones': Environmental (In)Justice in Helena María Viramontes's *Under the Feet of Jesus.*" *Interdisciplinary Studies in Literature and Environment* 12 (Winter 2005): 61–78.

Gruesser, John Cullen, ed. *The Unruly Voice: Rediscovering Pauline Elizabeth Hopkins*. Urbana: U of Illinois P, 1996.

Harrison, Lawrence. "The End of Multiculturalism." *Christian Science Monitor* 26 Feb. 2008.

Hitchens, Christopher. *God Is Not Great: How Religion Poisons Everything*. New York: Twelve, 2007.

Hofrichter, Richard. Introduction. *Toxic Struggles: The Theory and Practice of Environmental Justice*. Ed. Richard Hofrichter. Salt Lake City: U of Utah P, 2002. 1–10.

Hogan, Linda. *Dwellings: A Spiritual History of the Living World*. New York: Norton, 1995.

hooks, bell. *Teaching to Transgress: Education as the Practice of Freedom*. New York: Routledge, 1994.

Hopkins, Pauline Elizabeth. "Address at the *Citizens' William Lloyd Garrison Centenary Celebration*." *Daughter of the Revolution: The Major Nonfiction Works of Pauline E. Hopkins*. Ed. Ira Dworkin. New Brunswick, NJ: Rutgers UP, 2007. 355–57.

———. "Monroe Rogers." *Daughter of the Revolution: The Major Nonfiction Works of Pauline E. Hopkins*. Ed. Ira Dworkin. New Brunswick, NJ: Rutgers UP, 2007. 269–76.

———. *Winona, a Tale of Negro Life in the South and Southwest*. *The Magazine Novels of Pauline Hopkins*. Ed. Hazel V. Carby. New York: Oxford UP, 1988.

Hughes, Langston. Introduction. *Uncle Tom's Cabin*. By Harriet Beecher Stowe. New York: Dodd, Mead, 1952. i–iii.

Jameson, Fredric. *Postmodernism, or, The Cultural Logic of Late Capitalism*. Durham, NC: Duke UP, 2005.

Johnson, James Weldon. "Perverted History." *The Selected Writings of James Weldon Johnson*. Ed. Sondra Wilson. New York: Oxford UP, 1995. 156–57.

Johnson, Linck C. "A Week on the Concord and Merrimack Rivers." *The Cambridge Companion to Henry David Thoreau*. Ed. Joel Myerson. Cambridge: Cambridge UP, 1995. 40–56.

Kelley, Robin D. G. *Yo' Mama's Disfunktional! Fighting the Culture Wars in Urban America*. Boston: Beacon P, 1997.

Kingsolver, Barbara. *Animal, Vegetable, Miracle: A Year of Food Life.* New York: HarperCollins, 2007.

Kivel, Paul. *Uprooting Racism: How White People Can Work for Racial Justice.* Gabriola Island, BC: New Society, 2002.

Klindienst, Patricia. *The Earth Knows My Name: Food, Culture, and Sustainability in the Gardens of Ethnic Americans.* Boston: Beacon, 2006.

Klinkenborg, Verlyn. "Our Vanishing Night." *National Geographic Magazine* Nov. 2008: 102–23.

Kolodny, Annette. *The Lay of the Land: Metaphor as Experience and History in American Life and Letters.* Chapel Hill: U of North Carolina P, 1984.

———. "Tenure, Academic Freedom, and the Career I Once Loved." *Academe* 94 (2008): 22–26.

Kovel, Joel. *The Enemy of Nature: The End of Capitalism or the End of the World?* New York: Zed, 2007.

Kronman, Anthony T. *Education's End: Why Our Colleges and Universities Have Given Up on the Meaning of Life.* New Haven, CT: Yale UP, 2007.

LaDuke, Winona. *Recovering the Sacred: The Power of Naming and Claiming.* Cambridge, MA: South End, 2005.

———. "A Society Based on Conquest Cannot Be Sustained: Native Peoples and the Environmental Crisis." *Toxic Struggles: The Theory and Practice of Environmental Justice.* Ed. Richard Hofrichter. Salt Lake City: U of Utah P, 2002. 98–106.

Lauter, Paul. *From Walden Pond to Jurassic Park: Activism, Culture, & American Studies.* Durham, NC: Duke UP, 2001.

———. Introduction. *Walden* and *Civil Disobedience.* New York: Houghton Mifflin, 2000. 1–12.

Lee, Su-Im. "'We Are Not the World': Global Village, Universalism, and Karen Tei Yamashita's *Tropic of Orange.*" *Modern Fiction Studies* 53 (2007): 501–27.

Lerner, Michael. *The Left Hand of God: Taking Back Our Country from the Religious Right.* San Francisco: HarperCollins, 2006.

Lim, Shirley Geok-lin, María Herrera-Sobek, and Genara Padilla, eds. *Power, Race, and Gender in Academe: Strangers in the Tower.* New York: MLA, 1999.

López, Ian Haney. *White by Law: The Legal Construction of Race.* New York: NYU P, 1996.

Lorde, Audre. "The Master's Tools Will Never Dismantle the Master's House." *Sister Outsider: Essays and Speeches.* Berkeley, CA: Crossing, 1984. 110–13.

———. "The Uses of Anger." *Sister Outsider: Essays and Speeches.* Berkeley, CA: Crossing, 1984. 124–33.

Lydersen, Kari. "Climate Warming Linked to Illness." *Boston Globe* 21 Oct. 2008: A6.

Maathai, Wangari. "The Linkage between Patenting of Life Forms, Genetic Engineering and Food Security." *CropChoice News* 17 Oct. 2004. Web. 2008. http://www.genetinfo.org/documents/AfricaGMOsPatents.pdf.

McIntosh, Peggy. "White Privilege: Unpacking the Invisible Knapsack." *Race, Class, and Gender in the United States: An Integrated Study.* 4th ed. Ed. Paula S. Rothenberg. New York: St. Martin's, 1998. 165–69.

Mena, María Cristina. *The Collected Stories of María Cristina Mena.* Ed. Amy Doherty. Houston: Arte Público, 1997.

Michaels, Walter Benn. *The Trouble with Diversity: How We Learned to Love Identity and Ignore Inequality.* New York: Henry Holt, 2006.

Mohanty, Satya P. *Literary Theory and the Claims of History: Postmodernism, Objectivity, Multicultural Politics.* Ithaca, NY: Cornell UP, 1997.

Monbiot, George. *Heat: How to Stop the Planet from Burning.* Cambridge, MA: South End, 2007.

Moody, Joycelyn. *Sentimental Confessions: Spiritual Narratives of Nineteenth-Century African American Women.* Athens: U of Georgia P, 2000.

Morrison, Toni. *Playing in the Dark: Whiteness and the Literary Imagination.* Cambridge, MA: Harvard UP, 1990.

Morton, Timothy. *Ecology without Nature.* Cambridge, MA: Harvard UP, 2007.

Moya, Paula M. *Learning from Experience: Minority Identities, Multicultural Struggles.* Berkeley: U of California P, 2002.

Muller, Marlene, and Dennis Vogt. "In the Service of Hope — A Conversation with Wendell Berry." *Conversations with Wendell Berry.* Ed. Morris Allen Grubbs. Jackson: UP of Mississippi, 2007. 201–14.

Myers, Jeffrey. *Converging Stories: Race, Ecology, and Environmental Justice in American Literature*. Athens: U of Georgia P, 2005.

Naylor, Gloria. *Mama Day*. New York: Vintage, 1989.

Nordhaus, Ted, and Michael Shellenberger. *Break Through: From the Death of Environmentalism to the Politics of Possibility*. Boston: Houghton Mifflin, 2007.

O'Connell, Barry. Introduction. *On Our Own Ground: The Complete Writings of William Apess, a Pequot*. Amherst: U of Massachusetts P, 1992. xiii–lxxvii.

Oliner, Pearl, and Samuel Oliner. *Toward a Caring Society: Ideas into Action*. Westport, CT: Praeger, 1995.

*Oriental, or, Tung-Ngai San-Luk* 1 Feb. 1855.

Orr, David W. *Earth in Mind: On Education, Environment, and the Human Prospect*. Washington, DC: Island, 1994.

Ortiz, Simon J. *Men on the Moon*. Tucson: U of Arizona P, 1999.

———. "Towards a National Indian Literature: Cultural Authenticity in Nationalism." *MELUS* 8 (Summer 1981): 7–12. Rpt. in *American Indian Literary Nationalism*. Ed. Jace Weaver, Craig S. Womack, and Robert Warrior. Albuquerque: U of New Mexico P, 2005. 253–60.

Paredes, Raymond A. "Mexican-American Literature: An Overview." *Recovering the U.S. Hispanic Literary Heritage*. Ed. Ramón Gutiérrez and Genaro Padilla. Houston: Arte Público, 1993. 31–51.

Peltier, Leonard. "Peltier Statement for the 2008 Oglala Commemoration." Web. http://www.FreePeltierNow.org. 27 June 2008.

———. *Prison Writings: My Life Is My Sun Dance*. New York: St. Martin's Griffin, 1999.

Perry, Ruth. "Engendering Environmental Thinking: A Feminist Analysis of the Present Crisis." *Yale Journal of Criticism* 6 (1993): 1–16.

"Pew Forum Survey." *Boston Globe* 24 June 2008: A1, A8.

Pfister, Joel. "Complicity Critiques." *American Literary History* 12 (Fall 2000): 610–32.

Plumwood, Val. *Environmental Culture: The Ecological Crisis of Reason*. London: Routledge, 2002.

Robinson, Marilynne. *Housekeeping*. New York: Farrar, Straus and Giroux, 1980.

Roppolo, Kimberly. "Vision, Voice, and Intertribal Metanarrative: The American Indian Visual-Rhetorical Tradition and Leslie Marmon Silko's *Almanac of the Dead*." *American Indian Quarterly* 31.4 (2007): 534–58.

Rose, Wendy. *Bone Dance: New and Selected Poems, 1965–1993*. Tucson: U of Arizona P, 1994.

———. "The Great Pretenders: Further Thoughts on White Shamanism." *The State of Native America: Genocide, Colonization, and Resistance*. Ed. M. Annette Jaimes. Boston: South End, 1992. 403–21.

Roy, Modhumita. "Immaculate Conception: Outsourcing Reproductive Labour and Questions for Feminist Analysis." The MacMillan-Stewart Lecture on Women in the Developing World. Massachusetts Institute of Technology, Cambridge, 30 Oct. 2008.

Ruffin, Kimberly. *Black on Earth: African Americans and Ecological Insights*. Athens: U of Georgia P, 2010.

Sanders, Scott Russell. *A Conservationist Manifesto*. Bloomington: Indiana UP, 2009.

Seager, Joni. "Patriarchal Vandalism: Militaries and the Environment." *Dangerous Intersections: Feminist Perspectives on Population, Environment, and Development*. Ed. Jael Silliman and Ynestra King. Cambridge, MA: South End, 1998.

Sedensky, Matt. "Graham Kin to Lead Church." *Baton Rouge Advocate* 16 Mar. 2009: 8A.

Shiva, Vandana. *Earth Democracy: Justice, Sustainability, and Peace*. Cambridge, MA: South End, 2005.

———. *Soil Not Oil*. Cambridge, MA: South End, 2008.

Silko, Leslie Marmon. *Almanac of the Dead*. New York: Simon and Schuster, 1991.

———. "Notes from the Author." New York: Simon and Schuster, n.d.

Smith, Andrea. *Native Americans and the Christian Right: The Gendered Politics of Unlikely Alliances*. Durham, NC: Duke UP, 2008.

Spalding, Matthew. "The Case for Patriotic Assimilation." *Insider: Conservative Solutions for Advancing Liberty* Summer/Fall 2006: 20–25.

Spang, Bently. "Colloquium." The Eighth Annual Native American Speakers Series at Tufts. Medford, MA, 9 Nov. 2007.

Stewart, James Brewer. *Holy Warriors: The Abolitionists and American Slavery*. New York: Hill and Wang, 1996.

Stowe, Harriet Beecher. *A Key to Uncle Tom's Cabin; Presenting the Original Facts and Documents upon Which the Story Is Founded*. Boston: J. P. Jewett, 1853.

———. *Uncle Tom's Cabin; or, Life Among the Lowly*. 1852. Ed. Elizabeth Ammons. 2nd ed. New York: W. W. Norton, 2009.

Szasz, Andrew. "The Dangerous Delusions of 'Inverted Quarantine.'" *Chronicle of Higher Education* 25 Jan. 2008: B12.

Takaki, Ronald T. *A Different Mirror: A History of Multicultural America*. Boston: Little, Brown, 1993.

Tatum, Beverly Daniel. "Talking about Race, Learning about Racism: The Application of Racial Identity Development Theory in the Classroom." *Facing Racism in Education*. 2nd ed. Ed. Tamara Beauboeuf-Lafontant and D. Smith Augustine. Cambridge, MA: Harvard Educational Review, 1996. 321–48.

Taylor, Clyde. *The Mask of Art: Breaking the Aesthetic Contract — Film and Literature*. Bloomington: Indiana UP, 1998.

Thoreau, Henry David. *Civil Disobedience*. *Walden* and *Civil Disobedience*. Ed. Paul Lauter. New York: Houghton Mifflin, 2000. 15–36.

———. "A Plea for John Brown." *The Writings of Henry David Thoreau*. Vol. 4. Boston: Houghton Mifflin, 1906. 409–40.

———. "Slavery in Massachusetts." *The Writings of Henry David Thoreau*. Vol. 4. Boston: Houghton Mifflin, 1906. 388–408.

———. *Walden*. *Walden* and *Civil Disobedience*. Ed. Paul Lauter. New York: Houghton Mifflin, 2000. 38–264.

Tomasky, Michael. *Left for Dead*. New York: Macmillan, 1996.

Tompkins, Jane. *Sensational Designs: The Cultural Work of American Fiction, 1790–1860*. New York: Oxford UP, 1986.

Treat, James, ed. *Native and Christian: Indigenous Voices on Religious Identity in the United States and Canada*. New York: Routledge, 1996.

Vallely, Paul. "Climate Change: How Poorest Suffer Most." *Independent* 28 Nov. 2007.

Viramontes, Helena María. *Under the Feet of Jesus*. New York: Penguin, 1996.

Wa, Hab, and Long Achick. *An Analysis of the Chinese Question, Consisting of A Special Message of the Governor, and, In Reply Thereto, Two Letters of the Chinamen, and A Memorial of the Citizens of San Francisco*. San Francisco: San Francisco Herald Printing Office, 1852.

Walker, David. *Appeal, in Four Articles; Together with A Preamble, To the Coloured Citizens of the World, but In Particular, and Very Expressly, To Those of the United States of America*. 3rd ed. 1830. New York: Hill and Wang, 1965.

Wallis, Jim. *God's Politics: Why the Right Gets It Wrong and the Left Doesn't Get It*. San Francisco: HarperSanFrancisco, 2005.

———. *The Soul of Politics: Beyond "Religious Right" and "Secular Left."* New York: Harcourt Brace, 1995.

Warrior, Robert Allen. "Canaanites, Cowboys, and Indians: Deliverance, Conquest, and Liberation Theology Today." *Native and Christian: Indigenous Voices on Religious Identity in the United States and Canada*. Ed. James Treat. New York: Routledge, 1996. 93–104.

———. *The People and the Word: Reading Native Nonfiction*. Minneapolis: U of Minnesota P, 2005.

Weaver, Jace, Craig S. Womack, and Robert Warrior. *American Indian Literary Nationalism*. Albuquerque: U of New Mexico P, 2005.

Weissman, Robert. "Corporate Plundering of Third-World Resources." *Toxic Struggles: The Theory and Practice of Environmental Justice*. Ed. Richard Hofrichter. Salt Lake City: U of Utah P, 2002. 186–96.

West, Cornel. *Democracy Matters: Winning the Fight against Imperialism*. New York: Penguin, 2004.

———. *Keeping the Faith: Philosophy and Race in America*. New York: Routledge, 1993.

———. *Prophetic Reflections: Notes on Race and Power in America*. Monroe, ME: Common Courage, 1993.

White, Evelyn C. "Black Women and the Wilderness." *The Stories That Shape Us — Contemporary Women Write about the West*. Ed. Theresa Jordan and James Hepworth. New York: Norton, 1995. 376–83.

White, Lynn, Jr. "The Historical Roots of Our Ecologic Crisis." *Science* 155 (1967): 1203–07. Rpt. in *The Ecocriticism Reader: Landmarks in Literary*

*Ecology.* Ed. Cheryll Glotfelty and Harold Fromm. Athens: U of Georgia P, 1996. 3–14.

Whitt, Laurie Anne. "Cultural Imperialism and the Marketing of Native America." *Contemporary Native American Cultural Issues.* Ed. Duane Champagne. Walnut Creek, CA: AltaMira, 1999. 169–92.

Williams, Raymond. *The Sociology of Culture.* 1981. Chicago: U of Chicago P, 1995.

Wills, John S. "Who Needs Multicultural Education? White Students, U.S. History, and the Construction of a Usable Past." *Anthropology and Education Quarterly* 27 (1996): 365–89.

Winant, Howard. *Racial Conditions: Politics, Theory, Comparisons.* Minneapolis: U of Minnesota P, 1994.

Yaeger, Patricia. "The Death of Nature and the Apotheosis of Trash; or, Rubbish Ecology." *PMLA* 123 (Mar. 2008): 321–39.

Yamashita, Karen Tei. *Tropic of Orange.* Minneapolis: Coffee House, 1997.

Yamato, Gloria. "Racism: Something about the Subject Makes It Hard to Name." *Race, Class, and Gender in the United States: An Integrated Study.* 4th ed. Ed. Paula S. Rothenberg. New York: St. Martin's, 1998. 150–53.

Zinn, Howard. *A People's History of the United States: 1492–Present.* New York: HarperCollins, 1999.

# Index